Pirchei Publishing
164 Village Path / P.O. Box 708
Lakewood, New Jersey 08701
(732) 370-3344
www.shulchanaruch.com

Product Produced & Compiled by YPS:
Rabbi Shaul Danyiel & Rabbi Ari Montanari
www.lionsden.info/YPS

THE YESHIVA PIRCHEI SHOSHANIM SHULCHAN ARUCH LEARNING
PROJECT

The Noahide Laws – Lesson Twenty Two

164 Village Path, Lakewood NJ 08701 732.370.3344
164 Rabbi Akiva, Bnei Brak, 03.616.6340

Outline of This Lesson:

1. Introduction

2. Classic *Semikhah*

3. Modern *Semikhah*

4. Problems With Modern *Semikhah*

5. Choosing a Rabbi

6. Kabbalah – Specialized Licenses

7. Honor Due to Torah Scholars

8. Honor Due to Torah Books

Selecting a Rabbi

Lesson

22

Introduction

In previous lessons we examined the laws governing what Torah may be learned by non-Jews and what Torah may be taught to non-Jews by Jews. In this final lesson on Torah study, we are going to look at Rabbis, different types of Rabbis, and the requirement to show proper honor to Torah scholars and Torah books.

Rabbinic Ordination: Classical *Semikhah*

And Moses spoke to the Lord, saying: 'Let the Lord, the God of all flesh, set a man over the congregation, who may go out before them, and who may come in before them, and who may lead them out, and who may bring them in; that the congregation of the Lord be not as sheep which have no shepherd.' And the Lord said unto Moses: "Take Joshua the son of Nun, a man in whom is spirit, and lay your hand upon him; and set him before Eleazer the priest, and before all the congregation; and give him a charge in their sight. And you shall put of your honor upon him that all the congregation of the children of Israel may hear. And he shall stand before Eleazer the priest, who shall inquire for him by the judgment of the Urim before the Lord; at his word shall they go out, and at his word they shall come in, both he, and all the children of Israel with him, even all the congregation.' And Moses did as the Lord commanded him; and he took Joshua, and set him before Eleazer the priest, and before the entire congregation. And he laid his hands upon him, and gave him a charge, as the Lord spoke by the hand of Moses.[1]

And Joshua the son of Nun was full of the spirit of wisdom; for Moses had laid his hands upon

---

[1] Numbers 27:15-23.

him; and the children of Israel hearkened unto him, and did as the Lord commanded Moses.[2]

And the God said to Moses: 'Gather unto Me seventy men of the elders of Israel, whom you know to be the elders of the people and officers over them; and bring them to the tent of meeting, that they may stand there with you. And I will come down and speak with you there; and I will take of the spirit which is upon you, and will put it upon them; and they shall bear the burden of the people with you, so that you should not have to bear it alone.[3]

The "laying on of hands" and "placing the spirit" described in the above verses are the first examples Rabbinic ordination and the beginning of classical *Semikhah* (*Semikhah* is Hebrew for ordination). Joshua went on to ordain others, who in-turn taught and ordained their students down through the generations. This ordination was not a license to teach Torah or to lead a congregation – it was the transferring of divinely sanctioned authority from one scholar to another. This ordination imbued the holder with a spirit of wisdom, imparting holiness to his words and thoughts. *Semikhah* was required for certain roles; it was especially needed in order to serve in the Sanhedrin and other institutions of Torah law. Upon entry of the Jewish people into Israel, certain rules took effect governing how this ordination was given[4]:

- *Semikhah* could only be conveyed by a quorum of three judges, one of whom must himself have *Semikhah*.[5] *Semikhah* could be conferred verbally or in writing. The "laying on of hands" was only practiced in the earlier generations. It was not practiced beyond the generation of Moses and Joshua.

- Both the grantor and recipient must be in Israel at the time *Semikhah* is given.

- In order to receive *Semikhah*, one must be an expert in all areas of Torah law. He must also be of proper character and zealously observant of the mitzvos and words of the sages.

An important detail of rabbinic ordination is that it was tiered: ordination was given in specific areas of Torah knowledge. To receive any one of these ordinations, however, a scholar must be capable and fluent in all areas of Torah knowledge. The ordinations were, in ascending degrees:[6]

---

[2] Deuteronomy 34:9.

[3] Numbers 11:16-17.

[4] Most of this material is taken from Maimonides, *Hil. Sanhedrin* 4.

[5] *Sanhedrin* 13b-14a. *Hilchos Sanhedrin* 4:5.

[6] *Sanhedrin* 5a.

- *Yoreh Yoreh* (He shall instruct, he shall instruct) – This ordination was for matters of religious and ritual law.

- *Yadin Yadin* (He shall judge, he shall judge) – This ordination qualified the scholar to matters of civil, criminal, and monetary law.

- *Yatir Yatir* or *Yatir Bechoros Yatir* (He shall permit, he shall permit) – This ordination qualified its holder to rule on matters of animal sacrifices and ritual purity.

This chain of ordination passed unbroken for centuries until shortly after the Bar Kokhba rebellion (132 – 135 CE). In the wake of Bar Kokhba's failed attempt to re-establish Jewish autonomy, the Romans viewed *Semikhah* as a dangerous expression of the Jewish desire for self-rule. They also realized that, by ending *Semikhah*, they would destroy the Sanhedrin. What ensued was a brutal program of persecution and suppression. By imperial decree, giving *Semikhah* was made a capital offense with terrible consequences. Not only were the parties to the *Semikhah* executed, but absolute destruction was decreed for the city in which *Semikhah* was granted. To emphasize his point, the emperor also ordered the complete destruction of all villages and settlements located within 2000 *Amos* of that city's boundaries.[7]

By the fourth and fifth centuries the Romans had driven most of the rabbinic community across the border into what is now Iraq. With few sages remaining in Israel, the chain of *Semikhah* eventually broke.[8] For the next several centuries, the title "rabbi" would not be used.[9] Instead, a scholar would either be referred to as "*khokham*" (wise one) or, if he held a position of authority, as a *Gaon* (eminence).

Rabbinic Ordination: Modern *Semikhah*

In modern times, *Semikhah* refers to a degree or diploma certifying one as having completed a course of study in halakhah, Jewish law. The impetus for this new *Semikhah* was the rise of the medieval university, which began to issue diplomas and degrees. Jewish communities, in constant flux, saw the value of credentialing its religious scholars. They called this academic degree *Semikhah* in

---

[7] *Sanhedrin* 14a.

[8] There are some Gaonic traditions indicating that ordination may have continued beyond the fourth century. See the *Kovetz Shaarei Tzedek*, p. 29-30 and *Sefer HaShtarot*, p. 132. However, even these concur that there is no modern *Semikhah*.

[9] The term "Rabbi" is not all that common in the Talmud either. There are many honorifics used in the Talmud for Torah scholars. However, most of them are referred to simply by their names or sobriquets.

commemoration of the classical *Semikhah*. While this *Semikhah* caught on in the European Jewish world, Sephardic communities did not adopt it until very late.

Today, *Semikhah* is given at three levels:

- **Rav U-Manhig** – The equivalent of a Bachelor's degree, this *Semikhah* originated in the 20th century at Ner Israel Rabbinical College in Baltimore, MD. It certifies the holder as a teacher and as knowing the basic laws of the synagogue ritual service and observance of the holidays. Not all yeshivas issue this *semikhah* or accept it as valid. Where accepted, the holder may use the title Rabbi.

- **Yoreh Yoreh** – Equivalent of a Master's degree. Based on the *classical Yoreh Yoreh,* this is usually awarded following a course of study in kashrus (dietary laws), Shabbat, *Niddah* (laws pertaining to married women), and *Aveilus* (mourning). Traditionally, the final exam is given in *Issur ve-heter* (a very detailed sub-section of the dietary laws). This is the most common *Semikhah* today. A Rabbi with this *Semikhah*, who holds a position of communal authority, may be called Rav.

- **Yadin Yadin** – Also based on the classical *Semikhah*, this ordination is the equivalent of a Ph.D. It requires extensive study of the laws of monetary and civil damages, as well as the laws of marriage and divorce. One who holds this ordination may be called a Rav or Dayan. In the US, however, they are usually called Rabbi or Rav.

There is a fourth level that is very uncommon in our times called *heter horaah* (although this term is confusingly applied to other ordinations as well) or *Semikhahs Moreh Horaah*. This is an all-encompassing *Semikhah* awarded to rare scholars who have mastered the entire body of Torah literature. Very few people receive this today.

The Problems with Modern *Semikhah*

Students of Judaism and Noahism should be aware that there are many details (and problems) with modern S*emikhah*:

- *Semikhah* is first and foremost a certification in Torah Law. Biblical interpretation, philosophy, and theology, are rarely, if ever, part of the curriculum. *Semikhah* is only relevant to the study of Torah law – it is not awarded for knowledge of other areas.

- *Semikhah* is an academic degree attained after a course of study and examination. It is not awarded based on righteousness or character. There are people with *Semikhah* who are not particularly pleasant.

- One who has *Semikhah* at one level may not teach or answer questions about law from a higher level. Someone with *Yoreh Yoreh* should not answer questions about *Yadin Yadin* material.

- In the past 15 or 20 years, many yeshivas have begun awarding *semikhahs* in very specific areas of study. For example, someone may take a course in the laws of *Shabbos* and receive *semikhah* in *Shabbos* (this may even be done online). However, he may not know any other area of Torah law.

- Such a person must be very cautious about holding himself out as a Rabbi because he is not qualified to discuss anything other than the laws of Shabbat. There are many "area specific" Rabbis in the world today. Unfortunately, many hold themselves out as "Torah authorities" when, in actuality, they are woefully unqualified outside their narrow area of study. Of Rabbis who teach or rule on matters in which they are not thoroughly versed, Maimonides describes them as "evil, arrogant people."[10]

- Because it is possible to get *Semikhah* in only one narrow area, it means that one does have to be a Torah scholar anymore to be a Rabbi. Likewise, one doesn't need to be a rabbi to be a Torah scholar.

- One does not have to study at a yeshiva to attain *Semikhah*. Either a person can study at a yeshiva and receive *Semikhah* from the Yeshiva, or one can study privately and be examined by a renowned Torah scholar.

Ultimately, the world of Torah scholarship is a meritocracy – the greater scholars receive the greatest recognition and are accorded authority on the merits of their achievements. For this reason, many of the greatest Torah scholars and authorities of the past 150 years never bothered with *Semikhah*.

Choosing a Rabbi

The only qualified Rabbis are those who are observant and received their training from orthodox institutions. If someone was ordained as a reform Rabbi, and subsequently became orthodox, their ordination remains invalid.

Know from where a Rabbi received *Semikhah*. Did he get it online, from a recognized Torah scholar, or from a Yeshiva? All three could be valid, depending

---

[10] *Hilchos Talmud Torah* 5:30.

on the source.

Also, what did the Rabbi have to study to receive his *Semikhah*? Was it one area (i.e. *Issur v'Heter*) or did he have to complete a long course of study? Most importantly – is the rabbi affiliated with a particular institution, or is he a "lone wolf?" "Lone wolf" rabbis who "do their own thing" should generally be avoided because they have no accountability to anyone other than themselves.

You must endeavor to find a Rabbi in whose scholarship you have confidence and who you believe will take your interests seriously. If you always agree with everything your Rabbi tells you, then your relationship with the rabbi is not healthy for you. You want to find a Rabbi who challenges you. Most important of all, you must find a Rabbi who is consistent in his teachings. A rabbi who changes his opinions to suit the audience at hand, or when he is challenged, should be avoided.

Kabbalah – License

Besides ordination, there is another rabbinic credentialing called *kabbalah* – although this is similar to the Hebrew word for mysticism, it has an entirely different meaning here. A *kabblah* is a license to practice as a *mohel* (perform circumcision), *Sofer* (scribe) or *Shochet* (kosher slaughterer).

- **Mohel** – An unlicensed *mohel* should not be used. Additionally, unlicensed *mohalim* are exposed to tremendous liability. Besides the religious requirement for licensure, many countries have laws that enforce certification.

- **Sofer** – There is a tremendous number of unlicensed *soferim* (scribes) today. Many of these are producing non-kosher *mezuzos* and *Tefillin*. Without licensure, their work would still remain unacceptable because the work of an unlicensed *Sofer* (scribe) considered non-kosher even if the unlicensed Sofer is a Torah scholar and if their work is executed properly. Purchase of *safrus* from an unlicensed person is likewise prohibited.

- **Shochet** (a ritual slaughterer of animals) – The requirement of licensure for *shochtim* is very stringent. The meat of an unlicensed *Shochet* is treated as non-kosher even if he slaughtered the animal correctly. As a result the meat is either discarded or sold to non-Kosher meat companies.

Honor Due to Torah Scholars

Rise before an elderly person and stand before a wise man.[11]

This teaches that we are obligated to show honor to a Torah scholar by standing in his presence. We must stand when a scholar enters or leaves a room if he is within six feet of us. For an exceptional scholar, we stand when he enters the room even from more than 6 feet away.

The Honor Due to Torah Books

There are a number of rules that ensure the respectful treatment of holy books. The *Kitzur Shulchan Aruch* (Concise Code of Jewish Law), 28:4 to 10, summarizes these:

28:4 One should treat sacred books, even those other than a Torah scroll, with great respect. If placed on a bench, it is forbidden to sit on this bench unless the texts are placed on some object whose height is at least a handbreadth. It is surely forbidden to place such texts on the ground. A person should not put a sacred text on his lap and rest his arms upon it. When necessary, one may sit on a chest that contains other sacred books. However, this is forbidden if it contains a Torah scroll. Chumashim {The writing of the five books of Moses} may be placed on books of the Prophets and Sacred Writings. Books of the Sacred Writings may be placed on books of the Prophets and books of the Prophets may be placed on books of the Sacred Writings. However, we may not place books of the Prophets or of the Sacred Writings on Chumashim.

28:5   A Torah scroll that has become worn should be placed in genizah. The same applies to other sacred texts, writings, and ritual articles. It is forbidden to burn them.

28:6   One should not toss sacred texts or even works of Law or Aggadah. Similarly, it is forbidden to turn them upside down. If one finds one upside down, he should turn it the right way up.

28:7   One should not urinate in the presence of holy texts. In an emergency, one should at the very least, see that they are placed ten handbreadths up.

28:8   One should not make covers or mantles for a sacred article, from an article that was used for ordinary purposes. However, ex post facto, it is permitted. However, if it was made from an article that was used for idol worship, even after the fact, it is forbidden.

---

[11] Leviticus 19:32.

28:9   It is forbidden to use a holy text for one's own benefit - e.g., to stand it up for shade in the sun, or as a screen so that his colleague does not see what he is doing. However, if the sun is shining too brightly on the text that one is studying, one may use another text for shade, because one is not using it for one's own benefit. Similarly, to place a sacred text under another text from which one is studying to raise it, to make studying easier, is allowed. However, one should not place one text inside another, so that one will not need to search afterwards for the place one was learning. One should not rule a notebook on top of a sacred text since a notebook is not sacred until one has written in it. Similarly, one should not place paper and the like within a sacred text to be preserved.

28:10   One who destroys sacred texts transgresses a negative commandment, "Do not do so to the Lord, your God." We need to rebuke the binders of books, who (often) glue, in the covers of books, pages from sacred texts. Also great care should be taken when giving old holy texts to a gentile binder to rebind. One should remove the old covers and hide them, so the binder does not use them for secular books.

THE YESHIVA PIRCHEI SHOSHANIM SHULCHAN ARUCH LEARNING
PROJECT

The Noahide Laws – Lesson Twenty Three

164 Village Path, Lakewood NJ 08701 732.370.3344
164 Rabbi Akiva, Bnei Brak, 03.616.6340

Outline of This Lesson:

1. Sanhedrin 58b – The Prohibition

2. Sanhedrin 58b – Commentary

3. Yevamos 48b – Shabbat & the Ger Toshav

4. Talmud Krisus 9a – A Similar Conversation & Conclusion

5. The Midrash Rabbah Explains...

Shabbat I

Introduction

The question of Noahide observance of Shabbat comes up a lot. Unfortunately, there is much confusion surrounding the issue. Some have encouraged Noahides to keep a form of Shabbat observance, mistakenly equating Noahides with *ger toshav* (as well as erroneously understanding the *ger toshav's* relationship to Shabbat). This confusion is understandable considering that the question involves advanced mechanics of Torah law and a beguiling array of often contradictory sources.

Sanhedrin 58b – The Prohibition

Said Reish Lakish: A non-Jew who refrains from labor for an entire day is liable for death, as it is written:

> *"Day and night they shall not cease." (Genesis 8:22)*

The master said: Their warning is sufficient to warrant their death.

Said Ravina: This is so even if a non-Jew refrained from work on Monday.

[Challenge:] If this is so, then let this prohibition be counted among the Noahide laws!

[Answer:] The Noahide laws are enumerated as prohibitions. They are not listed according to their positive aspects.

Sanhedrin 58b – Commentary

Said <u>Reish Lakish</u>: *A non-Jew who refrains from labor for an entire day is liable for death, as it is written:*

> *"Day and night they shall not cease."(Genesis 8:22)*

Explanation: This verse, at first glance, seems to refer to the progress of the seasons. However, Reish Lakish explains the word "they" as referring to man. Therefore, this verse is prohibiting Noah and his descendants from disengaging in the labor of the world for an entire day. This is a positive commandment that precludes observance of Shabbat. There is ambiguity though, as to whether this is a general prohibition on cessation of work or a specific prohibition on doing so for religious reasons.

The master said: Their warning is sufficient to warrant their death.

Explanation: This is the general rule for the transgression of a Noahide commandment for which a warning is evidenced in the Torah.[1] Certain prohibitions, however, are derived obliquely and are not subject to punishment by death.[2] The Rambam understands the punishment for keeping Shabbat as heavenly and not imposed by human courts.

Said <u>Ravina</u>: *This is so even if a non-Jew refrained from work on Monday.*

Explanation: The intent of Ravina's statement is unclear.

Rashi[3], **Ridbaz**[4], **Rav Moshe**[5] - They understand Ravina as telling us that gentiles are prohibited from establishing a particular 24-hour period to abstain from work for any reason. To take a day off occasionally for rest only, with no religious motivation, would be acceptable, however.

---

[1] See <u>Hilchos Melakhim</u> 9:14.

[2] See <u>Hilchos Melakhim</u> 10:6.

[3] Ad loc.

[4] Commentary to Rambam, *Hilkhos Melachim 10:9.*

[5] *Igros Moshe YD* II: 9.

Yad Ramah[6] - This prohibition applies only if the rest is religiously motivated. It does not matter, according to them, whether this motivation is monotheistic or pagan. According to then, to establish a 24-hour period to rest from work for health reasons would be permitted.

[Challenge:] If this is so, then let this prohibition be counted among the Noahide laws!

[Answer:] The Noahide laws are enumerated as prohibitions. They are not listed according to their positive aspects.

Explanation: Rashi and other Talmudic commentaries explain that the Noahide laws, meaning the general categories themselves, are listed according to their negative *(thou shalt not)* aspects only. Even though the laws may include positive commandments, these are sub-classes of the general prohibitions. As mentioned in a previous lesson, *dinim* (the requirement to establish courts) appear to be positive. Nevertheless, it is primarily negative in that it establishes courts to enforce the other negative prohibitions.

Yevamos 48b – Shabbat and the Ger Toshav

Sanhedrin 58b is apparently contradicted by a *braisa* in Yevamos 48b. The Talmud there is discussing the laws of an *eved*, indentured servant, purchased before Shabbat and the prohibition of his performing work on behalf of his master. The same *braisa* concludes with a surprising statement:

*[Six days you shall work, but on the seventh day you shall rest. Your ox and donkey shall have rest, the son of your maidservant, **and the ger**, so that they may be refreshed. (Exodus 23:12)]*

"…and the ger"– *this refers to a* ger toshav *[resident alien].*

Explanation: Talmud tells us that the word *ger*, used in this verse, refers to a *ger toshav*. So, is this verse telling us that a *ger toshav* must observe Shabbat? How can that be? A *ger toshav* is not Jewish and, as the Talmud stated in Sanhedrin, non-Jews cannot observe Shabbat! Since the verse uses the generic term *ger*, it might be that the Torah means a *ger tzedek*, a convert to Judaism.

You might question: How do we know this refers to a ger toshav? *Perhaps it refers to a* ger tzedek, *[a regular convert to Judaism]? This cannot be so, because another verse states:*

---

[6] To Sanhedrin 58b.

And the Seventh day is a Sabbath… you shall do no labor… both you and the ger *within your gates.*
(Deuteronomy 5:14)

Explanation: The Talmud understands the verse *"ger* within your gates" as referring to a *ger tzedek* – a full convert to Judaism. Since another verse has already taught us that a *ger tzedek* must observe Shabbos as a Jew, then our passage must be referring to a *ger tzedek,* the only other type of *ger.*

What are we to make of this? There are a number of explanations:

- **Rashi** – Rashi understands the Talmud simply: A *ger toshav* must keep Shabbat. Apparently, Rashi derives his position this from the Talmud in <u>Eruvin 69b.</u> There it states that one who desecrates Shabbat is like one who worships idolatry. Rashi applies this idea to a *ger toshav.* Since the *ger toshav* has disavowed idolatry, he must therefore keep Shabbat. Rashi must interpret the Talmud's prohibition (from Sanhedrin 58a) as only precluding idolaters from observing Shabbat.

- <u>*Tosafos* **D. H. Zeh**</u> – A *ger toshav* has no obligation to observe Shabbat and may not do so because of the aforementioned passage from Sanhedrin. The Talmud here is only discussing whether or not a non-Jew may do work for a Jew on Shabbat. This certainly seems the intent of the verse:

  Six days you shall work, but on the seventh day you shall rest. Your ox and donkey shall have rest, the son of your maidservant, **and the** *ger, so that they may be refreshed*

  The first part of this verse discusses animals or servants working on behalf of a Jew (they clearly have no intrinsic obligation to observe Shabbat). Correspondingly, the first part of the *braisa* discusses a Jew's servant working on his behalf. The second part of the *braisa* is explaining that a *ger toshav* is likewise prohibited from working on behalf of a Jew.

The basis of Rashi and *Tosafos's* disagreement appears to be that the other entities mentioned in the verse (ox, donkey, servant, etc.) are subject to the will of a master, while the *ger toshav* is not. A *ger toshav* is completely autonomous. *Tosafos* seems to interpret the verse's inclusion of *ger toshav* to mean: "You may think that a *ger toshav,* being a non-Jew who is not in your household, may labor on your behalf, but the verse is teaching that this is not so."

Tosafos's explanation is certainly consistent with the Talmud's discussion. Rashi's opinion, though, is very difficult to understand. First of all, <u>*Eruvin* 69b</u> is only describing Jewish desecration of Shabbat, not that of a *ger toshav*. To apply it to a *ger toshav*, we have to have some other pre-existing reason to equate Jewish desecration of Shabbat to that of a *ger toshav*. Moreover, the comparison is made for the unique purposes of explaining when a Sabbath desecrating Jew may be trusted or combined with other Jews for certain matters of *halakha*. In other words, it is only asking when a Jew is treated as an idolater in certain areas of Torah law. This entire issue is compounded by the lack of clarity as to how Rashi defines *ger toshav*.

Because of the difficulties in explaining Rashi, the Maimonides,[7] <u>*Shulchan Aruch*</u>,[8] and all other codifiers[9] decide the <u>*halakha*</u> like *Tosafos*. Therefore, even a *ger toshav* is included in the prohibition of gentile observance of Shabbat.

Talmud *Krisus 9a*

There is similar discussion in the Talmud to Tractate *Krisus* 9a:

> *Our Rabbis taught [in a* braisa*]: A* ger toshav *does work for himself on Shabbat to the same degree as a Jew on the intermediate days of the festivals.[10]*

> <u>*Rabbi Akiva*</u> *said: As a Jew does on the festivals.[11]*

> <u>*Rabbi Yossi*</u> *said: A* ger toshav *does labor on Shabbat for himself just a Jew does on a weekday.*

> *Rabbi Shimon said: Both a* ger toshav*, an idolater, a resident slave, or maidservant do labor for themselves on Shabbat just as a Jew does on a weekday.*

The Talmud tells us that the *halakha* is like Rabbi Shimon.[12]

---

[7] Rambam, <u>*Hilkhos Shabbos* 20:14.</u>

[8] *Orach Chaim* 304.

[9] Ibid. See the <u>*Bais Yosef*</u> there for a lengthy discussion of the issues.

[10] On the intermediate days of the Passover and Sukkot festival Jews may only do labor that is needed for enjoyment of the festivals or to prevent a loss.

[11] On the festivals themselves Jews may cook as well as carry in the public domain.

[12] See emendations of the Shitta Mekubetzes here, note 12. See also Maimonides, Hilkhos Shabbos 20:14.

Thus far, we see have seen that there is nothing preventing a *ger toshav* from performing labor on Shabbat. Since a *ger toshav* is a de facto Noahide, we may infer that that there is nothing prohibiting a Noahide from doing labor on Shabbat.

At the same time, there is a positive commandment requiring the inhabitants of the world to constantly engage in the world. This requirement precludes observance of Shabbat.

Midrash Rabbah

The Midrash[13] explains the idea behind this prohibition:

> *Rabbi Yossi, son of Chanina, said: A gentile who observes the Shabbat before being circumcised is liable to the death penalty. Why? Because he was not so commanded. But, what is your reason for saying that a gentile who observes the Sabbath is liable to the death penalty? Said Rabbi Chiya, the son of Abba, in the name of Rabbi Yochanan: If a king and queen are sitting in conversation and someone comes and barges between them, isn't he liable to death? So too is the Shabbat between Israel and the Holy One, blessed is He, as it is written:*

> *"[You shall speak unto the Children of Israel, saying: you must keep my Shabbat, for it is a sign] between me and the Children of Israel" (Exodus 31:13).*

> *Therefore, a non-Jew who comes and places himself between them before being circumcised is liable to the death penalty.*

Prior to the giving of the Torah, the rest of Shabbat was the privilege of God alone and man was not allowed to partake it. The commandment of observing Shabbat, the divine day of rest, was given to the Jews alone as part of their unique covenant with God.

In the next lessons we will look at further possible relationships between Noahides and Shabbat.

Summary of Lesson

1. The Torah prohibits Noahides from observing Shabbat, requiring them to be involved constantly in the making of the world.

2. This prohibition only applies to religiously motivated resting.

---

[13] *Midrash Rabbah* to Deuteronomy 1:18.

3. A Ger Toshav has no obligation to observe Shabbat. They are likewise enjoined against observing Shabbat.

4. The Talmud in *Krisus* reiterates the Halakhah with regard to a ger toshav.

5. The Midrash Rabbah explains that the reason for the prohibition is because Shabbat is a matter between God and Israel alone.

THE YESHIVA PIRCHEI SHOSHANIM SHULCHAN ARUCH LEARNING PROJECT

The Noahide Laws – Lesson Twenty Four

164 Village Path, Lakewood NJ 08701 732.370.3344
164 Rabbi Akiva, Bnei Brak, 03.616.6340

Outline of This Lesson:

1. Introduction

2. Talmud *Yoma 28b*

3. 1) The Labor of Noahides

4. 2) The Definition of a Day

5. 3) The Circumstances of Pre-Sinaitic Noahides

6. 4) The Patriarchs & Monotheism

      a. In Summary

      b. *Yoma 28a*

      c. The *Binyan Tzion* Remains

7. Summary

Shabbat II: The Patriarchs & Shabbat

Introduction

In the last lesson we saw there is a positive *mitzvah* upon all non-Jews to remain constantly engaged with the world (*Sanhedrin* 58b). This *mitzvah*, by default, prohibits non-Jews from observing any 24 hour rest period for religious reasons (Maimonides). This law applies equally to all non-Jews, including *ger toshav* and Noahides (*Tosafos* to *Yevamos* 48b and *Kerisus* 9a).

We saw from the Midrash that the Jews were commanded to partake in the divine rest of Shabbat. Their observance of Shabbat was established as a sign of their unique covenant with God. Anyone else is an interloper and even deserving of death!

Yet, we are also taught that the patriarchs kept all of the *mitzvos*. This would, of course, include observing Shabbat. Considering that the patriarchs were Noahides, how do we reconcile their behavior with *halakhah*?

Talmud *Yoma* 28b

The source teaching us that the patriarchs kept the Torah is *Yoma* 28b:

> *Rav Said: Our forefather Avraham kept the entire Torah, as it is written:*
>
> *"Because Abraham obeyed My voice [and observed my safeguards, My commandments, My statutes, and my laws.]"*
>
> *Rav Shimi bar Chiya said to Rav: Why not say that verse speaks only of the seven Noahide laws?*

[Response]: It also referrers to circumcision, [therefore the verse must speak of more than just 7 laws.]

[Rav Simi bar Chiya responded]: Then say it refers only to the seven Noahide laws and to circumcision!

Rav said to him: If that were the case, then why does the verse state "My commandments... My laws?" This implies that Avraham kept the entire Torah.

Rav Ashi said: Our forefather Avraham fulfilled even eruvei tavshilin *[a rabbinic mitzvah] for it is stated "My Laws" [lit. "My Torahs"], implying both the written and oral Torahs[.]*

Many later commentaries hold like Rav Shimi bar Chiya, that the patriarchs only observed the Noahide laws plus the other *mitzvos* specifically commanded to them.[2] According to this understanding of the Talmud, the Patriarchs did not observe Shabbat.

There are a significant number of commentaries, however, who agree with Rav or Rav Ashi. According to them, the patriarchs observed the entire written Torah, oral Torah, and possible even later rabbinic decrees.[3]

Their view requires a lot of explanation. The most obvious question is: how did the patriarchs know the Torah before it was given? There are many good answers to this question, the most famous being that they knew it through *Ruach ha-kodesh*, a form of divine inspiration[4] just below prophecy.[5] This question, though, is nowhere nearly as difficult as the one posed by Leviticus 18:18:

Do not marry a woman and her sister...

Yet, Yaakov (Jacob) married two sisters (Rachel and Leah) despite this explicit Torah prohibition. How was this possible according to those who say that he

---

[1] Occasionally the term Oral Torah includes rabbinic decrees as well. See *Maharsha* and *Rashash*.

[2] See Rashbam, Chizkuni, Ibn Ezra and many others to Genesis 26:5. See the Meiri and Rabbi Avraham ben HaRambam in their introductions to *Pirkei Avos*. Maimonides in *Hilchos Melachim 9:1* holds similarly.

[3] See Responsa of Rashba I: 94 and Radbaz II: 696. This is also the opinion of Rashi. However their opinions are still somewhat circumscribed.

[4] Prophecy and inspiration will be discussed in a future lesson.

[5] Ramban to Genesis 26:5.

observed the entire Torah! There are many examples of patriarchal behavior appearing to contradict the Torah.[6]

According to the literalist interpretation of Rav and Rav Ashi, the Torah observance of the patriarchs must be somehow qualified to explain these contradictions. Many of the greatest Torah scholars in history have tackled this question and arrived at a number of solutions. For example:

- Ramban to Genesis 26:5 – The patriarchs only observed the Torah in the boundaries of Israel. This may be tied into their knowledge of the Torah via *Ruach haKodesh*.[7]

- The Maharal of Prague[8] writes that the Patriarchs only kept the positive commandments, not the negative commandments.

- The Rama[9] writes that there are indeed problems explaining how Yitzchak and Yaakov kept the Torah. His solution is to simply disagree with the early commentaries, writing that only Avraham kept the Torah. Indeed, the Talmud only states that Avraham kept the Torah before it was given. Almost all other commentaries disagree, holding that Yitzhak and Yaakov kept the mitzvos as well.

- *Ohr HaChaim* to Genesis 49:3 – Though they kept the Torah, it had not yet been revealed and was not, therefore, truly binding. Their observance of the Torah could be modified by prophecy. When they deviated from the Torah, it was due to prophetic instruction.

- *Daas Zekeinim* to Genesis 37:35 and *Nefesh HaChaim* 21 – since the Torah had not been given, the patriarchs had no actual obligation to observe it. The patriarchs were empowered to make judgment calls for the sake of building a people and community.

---

[6] For example, Amram, father of Moshe, married his aunt. Kayin married his sister. Problems are also caused by simple chronology. For example, how could the patriarchs have observed the laws of *Teruma* and *Ma'aser* if there were no Kohanim yet? How did the patriarchs observe laws dependent on future events, such as remembering the exodus from Egypt or the persecution of Amalek?

[7] As mentioned in a previous lesson, there is a special relationship between the land of Israel and the powers of prophecy and inspiration.

[8] *Gur Aryeh* to 46:10 and 32:4; *Chiddushei Aggados* Chullin 91a.

[9] Responsa 10.

This sampling reveals a trend: Most explanations of how the Patriarchs kept the Torah render their observance of Shabbat irrelevant to modern Noahides (see above, *Maharal, Ohr HaChaim, Daas Zekeinim,* and *Nefesh HaChaim*). A further problem is that many commentaries explain that the Patriarchs were not 100% Noahides.

Once they accepted the covenant of circumcision, the patriarchs were considered Jewish to a degree permitting them to partake in Shabbat.[10] This also precludes their observance from having any relevance to contemporary Noahides.

Therefore, to learn anything useful from the patriarchs, we must serious narrow our question. The exact question should be:

> How do we explain Shabbat observance of the Patriarchs according to those who hold that the Patriarchs were 100% Noahides and those who hold that they kept the Torah exactly as we understand "keeping the Torah?"

Although many have written about how the Patriarchs kept the Torah, the cross-section of those commentaries discussing our specific question is very small.

1) The Labor of Noahides

Let's look again at the verse prohibiting Noahide Shabbat observance:

> *Day and night they shall not cease...*

When the Torah prohibits gentiles from observing Shabbat, it is telling them that they may not refrain from labor for an entire day. What type of labor are we talking about, though? The *Binyan Tzion*[11] makes a brilliant observation. The 39 prohibited labors, the Torah's conception of labor for the purposes of Shabbat, were not articulated until Sinai. Since the details of these labors were not previously known to the world, they could not be definition of labor used in regard to Noahides and their prohibition of observing Shabbat.

For example, according to the 39 labors defined at Sinai, carrying a needle in the public domain is considered a prohibited labor for a Jew on Shabbat. However, if a Jew carries a sofa up and down the stairs of his home on Shabbat, it is not considered labor and is permitted.

---

[10] *Beit HaOtzar Maarekhet* I: 1; *Parshat Derakhim* 1. Rabbi Asher Weiss in *Minchas Asher* 9 records that this is the opinion of *HaRav HaGaon* Chaim Kanievsky.

[11] No. 126.

Before Sinai, however, the definition of labor was entirely colloquial. Therefore, the prohibition of observing Shabbat for gentiles was only on refraining from the colloquial definition of labor, not on the Jewish definition of labor. When the patriarchs rested, they observed the Torah (Jewish) definition of labor, which was not prohibited for them as Noahides. However, they did not refrain from colloquially defined forms of labor.

According to this understanding, gentiles are only enjoined against setting aside a day to refrain from their jobs, yard work, home repairs, etc. because of religious reasons. However, observing the Jewish definitions of labor for Shabbat is not a problem; it is not the type of labor from which they are prohibited from resting.

2) The Definition of Day

The _Panim Yafos_[12] also makes a remarkable observation. The verse states:

> _Day and night they shall not cease..._

This verse indicates that the Shabbat that may not be observed by non-Jews is one lasting from daybreak to daybreak. After all, the verse states _day and night_, not _night and day_. However, the Jewish Shabbat, the one commanded at Sinai, lasts from nightfall to nightfall. The patriarchs kept the Jewish Shabbat (nightfall to nightfall), which was never prohibited for gentiles.

This opinion would apparently permit Noahides to observe Shabbat in the same way as Jews. However, the _Panim Yafos's_ definition of "day" as daybreak-to-daybreak is disproven and rejected by numerous later authorities who find it at great variance with other established areas of _halakhah_.[13]

3) The Circumstances of Pre-Sinaitic Noahides

The Meiri[14] explains that the circumstances of the Patriarchs were fundamentally different from that of later Jews. He holds that the reason gentiles are prohibited from observing Shabbat is because a gentile is not permitted to imitate the Jewish faith. However, before the giving of the Torah, there were no Jews. Therefore, there is no point to prohibiting Shabbat observance.

---

[12] Commentary to Genesis 8:22.

[13] _Binyan Tzion_ 126; Responsa Rabbi Akiva Eiger 121 (Hosifos); Cheker Halakhah 15; Yad Shaul YD 293:4; Pardes Yosef, Noah 22; Teshuvos Toras Chesed 25.

[14] To _Sanhedrin_ 58b.

But, wait a minute, wasn't the key verse written in Genesis? This is long before the Jews were commanded to keep Shabbat. If there was no point at that time to prohibit non-Jewish Shabbat observance, then why is the verse written in Genesis?

The Meiri understands that it was written here for future generations. The Meiri would, therefore, prohibit any modern Noahide observance of Shabbat.

4) The Patriarchs & Monotheism

Rabbi Meir Dan Plotzki in his *Kuntres Ner Mitzvah*[15] offers an interesting and unexpected view. The Talmud states:[16]

> *Israel is not governed by* mazal.

Mazal is a broad term referring to the created agents and mediators (both angelic and physical) of God's providence in the world. It includes the motion of the stars and constellations and the physical and transcendent forces of the universe. These entities form a vast mechanism channeling God's providence into the world.

Before Sinai, all nations of the world were subjected to this mitigated divine providence. At Sinai, however, the Jews were taken out from this system and became subject to God's direct and unmitigated oversight. God signaled this new status by commanding the observance of Shabbat, by asking Israel to share in the divine rest of the seventh day. This is the intent of the verse:

> *Speak unto the children of Israel, saying: You must keep my Shabbat, for it is a sign between Me and you throughout your generations, that you may know that I am the Lord who sanctifies you. (Exodus 31:13)*

Given the Jews a portion in Shabbat was the sign that they were no longer subject to the cycles of time, seasons, and stars – the lesser providence.

The non-Jewish nations are subject to *mazal*, hence they must observe the cycle of time and days. When a non-Jew observes a religious Shabbat, it is an attempt to lay claim to the unique providence of Israel, to cast off the mitigating forces of creation. This is why the Midrash describes non-Jewish observance of Shabbat as an interposition between a king and queen – it is the usurping of a private, unique relationship.

---

[15] An important overview of the Noahide laws.

[16] *Shabbat* 156a and *Nedarim* 32a.

However, God commanded Avraham: *Exit from your stargazing! Israel is not governed by* mazal![17]

God was telling Avraham that, from that point onward, he would merit God's direct providence and no longer be subject to the influences of *mazal*. Therefore, Avraham was permitted to observe Shabbat fully.

The *Chemdas Yisrael* further explains that Abraham merited this providence by disavowing idolatry.

This explanation fits well with Rashi's opinion that a *ger toshav* must keep Shabbat (assuming Rashi defines a ger toshav as one who only does not worship idols).

However, it appears from the Talmud[18] that, assuming a change in providence is the underlying factor, this change only applied to Abraham and his descendants, but to none other.

Furthermore, this interpretation does not work according to *Tosafos* (which is the *halakha*), who holds that even a *ger toshav* may not keep Shabbat.

IN SUMMARY:

Binyan Tzion – Non-Jews are only prohibited from refraining from colloquially defined types of labor. They may choose to refrains from the 39 *Melachos*.

Panim Yafos – The prohibition is only on observing a Shabbat of daybreak-to-daybreak. However, the definition of "day" as daybreak-to-daybreak is difficult. His interpretation is rebutted by many later authorities.

Meiri – The Patriarchs were Noahides and did keep Shabbat. However, the prohibition against Shabbat observance did not apply at that time.

Chemdas Yisrael – Because they were not idolaters, the patriarchs merited God's direct providence. Shabbat is the sign of such providence. This interpretation is precluded by *Tosafos*, though, and from *Yoma* 28a.

YOMA 28A

Rav Safra Said: The time of the afternoon prayer of Avraham [minchah] is when the walls began to grow dark.

Rabbi Yosef said: We learn halakha *from Avrham! [Surprised objection]*

---

[17] *Shabbat* 156a and *Nedarim* 32a, based upon Genesis 15.

[18] Note 15, above.

Rabbeinu Tam, the *Aruch*, *Ritva*, *Maharitz Chayes*,[19] and many others explain that *halakha*, practice, cannot be learned based on the conduct of the patriarchs before the Torah was given.[20] God's expectations for the world and the way in which we relate to God fundamentally changed at Sinai.

Therefore, the *Chemdas Yisrael's* conclusion is not practical.

THE *BINYAN TZION* REMAINS

From the above opinions, only the *Binyan Tzion's* (regarding the nature of labor for Noahides) remains: the patriarchs kept the Jewish Shabbat yet engaged in the colloquial definition of labor.

This conclusion remains because it is a valid halakhic interpretation all to itself, and is not dependent on the behavior, status, or actions of the patriarchs.

However, it is virtually impossible to carry out this idea in practice. How does one keep the Shabbat according to the Jewish definition of labor while engaging in what is colloquially termed "work?" The two definitions overlap substantially. Additionally, observing the Jewish sabbatical restrictions may present a problem of *chiddushei dat*, which will be examined in the next lesson.

Summary of This Lesson

1. The Talmud tells us that the patriarchs kept the Torah before it was given at Sinai.

2. This cannot be taken 100% literally, because there are examples of the Patriarchs not following Torah laws.

3. To learn from the Patriarchs observance of Shabbat to modern Noahides, we have to look at commentaries that both view the Patriarchs as 100% Noahides and that hold their Torah observance was identical to ours. There are very, very few views satisfying these conditions.

4. Of those meeting our conditions, most of them do not apply to modern Noahides.

5. There is a general rule that we cannot learn our practice from the behavior of the Patriarchs.

---

[19] All commenting to this page of the Talmud.

[20] This is only a general rule that is not without its exceptions.

6. The *Binyan Tzion's* interpretation, however, may have relevance to modern Noahides. However, it is impossible to apply it in practice.

THE YESHIVA PIRCHEI SHOSHANIM SHULCHAN ARUCH LEARNING PROJECT

The Noahide Laws – Lesson Twenty Five

164 Village Path, Lakewood NJ 08701 732.370.3344
164 Rabbi Akiva, Bnei Brak, 03.616.6340

Outline of This Lesson:

1. Introduction & Review

2. Maimonides *Hilkhos Melakhim* 10:9

3. Rabbi Moshe Feinstein, *ztz"l*

4. In Conclusion

5. Letter of the Law vs. Spirit of the Law

6. Observance vs. Acknowledgement

7. Shabbat Suggestions

8. Summary

Shabbat III: Practical Conclusions

Introduction & Review Thus Far

This is a summary of what the sources have taught us so far:

- **Sanhedrin 58b** – Cites Genesis 8:22 which prohibits all mankind from keeping Shabbat. The verse prohibits cessation from work for a 24 hour period. Prior to Sinai, the respite of Shabbat was for God alone At Sinai, the Jews were commanded to partake in the experience of Shabbat as a sign of their unique status.

- **Rashi, Radbaz, Rav Moshe Feinstein** commenting on the **Rambam** – For the sake of this prohibition, it does not make difference as to why one rests for an entire day. Even if one sets aside an entire day only to recuperate from work, he still transgresses. The Radbaz clarifies, though, that this is only if one establishes a regular, fixed day. To take an occasional day off is permitted.

- **Midrash Rabba** – Explains that the prohibition of non-Jewish observance of Shabbat takes on special poignancy after the giving of the Torah. The Jews were commanded at Sinai to partake of the divine rest of Shabbat as a sign of their covenant. Anyone else who tries to do so is interposing between God and Israel.

- **The Patriarchs** – The patriarchs, we are taught, kept the Torah. However, both the nature of their observance and their identity as Noahides are not clear enough for us to draw any practical conclusions. Additionally, there is a principle that we do not learn *halakha*, practice, from the actions of the patriarchs.

Maimonides *Hilkhos Melakhim* 10 : 9

§9 *A non-Jew[1] who delves into the Torah is obligated to die. They should only be involved in the study of their seven commandments.*

Similarly, a non-Jew who rests, even on a weekday, observing that day similarly to a Shabbat, is obligated to die. Needless to say, this is also the case if he creates a festival for himself.

> In the Torah, the Hebrew word "Shabbat" may refer to the Shabbat, the seventh day, or any day upon which labor is prohibited by the Torah. This would include festivals. The Radbaz quotes Rashi who writes[2] that any kind of rest for any reason should be prohibited. However, the Radbaz adds "This is if he establishes a day for rest; however, occasional cessation from labor is not prohibited."

The general rule governing these matters is this: they may not originate a new religion or create/perform mitzvot *for themselves based on their own reasoning. Either convert and accept all the* mitzvot *or uphold their commandments without adding or detracting from them.*

> Maimonides explains that the reason for the prohibition of Shabbat observance by non-Jews is *chiddushei dat*, originating a new religion (discussed at length in a prior lesson). *Chiddushei dat* would preclude Noahides from observing Shabbat even by refraining from the Jewish definition of labor; the 39 *melachot*.

If a gentile delves into the Torah or Shabbat, or innovates a religious practice, he is beaten, punished, and informed him that he is obligated to die for his actions. However, he is not actually executed.

HaRav HaGaon Moshe Feinstein, *ztz"l*

Rabbi Moshe Feinstein[3] explains that *chiddushei dat* is a general prohibition against Noahides adopting Jewish practices as religious observances. However, the prohibition of observing Shabbat and the strictures on Torah study are singled out by Maimonides due to their severity.

---

[1] Many printed editions of the *Mishnah Torah*, being heavily censored, read *akum*, meaning *idolater*. However, almost all early manuscripts and critical editions read *goy*, a generic term for anyone who is not Jewish.

[2] Sanhedrin 58b.

[3] In a number of letters he discusses Noahide issues. See *Igros Moshe* OC II:25, V:18, YD I:3, I:6, II:7, II:8, III:90, IV:51:1, CM II:69.

In Conclusion

According to Maimonides, Noahides may also not observe Shabbat by refraining from the Jewish definition of work (the 39 *Melachos*). This would be *chiddushei dat*.

Chiddushei dat would also prohibit Noahides from marking Shabbat in anyway by using Jewish rituals such as lighting candles, making Kiddush, making the blessing for bread over two loaves, etc.

The conclusion of the *poskim* is, therefore, that Noahides may not observe Shabbat in anyway by refraining from work for a 24 hour period or by adopting Jewish rituals. Noahides may neither establish a regular 24-hour period of rest even for non-religious reasons.[4]

Letter of the Law vs. Spirit of the Law

A Noahide has two options as to how to deal with the question of labor on Shabbat. He may either take the liberal approach, which follows only the strict letter of the law, or he may take a pious, conservative approach acknowledging both the spirit and letter of the law.

The Letter of the Law

The letter of the law is that a Noahide may not commemorate Shabbat by regularly refraining from work for an entire day. It does not matter if one rests from daybreak-to-daybreak or from nightfall-to-nightfall. This approach implies that refraining from only some labors, or even from all labor but only part of the day, is not a problem. According to this approach, a Noahide should turn on a light, make a fire, write, or do at least one prohibited act so that his observance of Shabbat is not a complete observance. Otherwise he would transgress the prohibition of observing Shabbat.

We should keep in mind, though, that this observance of Shabbat is meaningless. "Observance" of Shabbat means resting from the 39 labors defined at Sinai. The purpose in a Noahide doing one prohibited labor is so that he does not run afoul of the prohibition of observing Shabbat. That means that his one-prohibited-labor invalidates the entire observance. Therefore, despite resting for a whole day, on account of the one labor he is required to do, he never kept Shabbat anyway!

Furthermore, as we mentioned earlier, God only asked Israel to share in Shabbat. A Noahide who does so is imposing his will upon God. As we saw in earlier lessons, this is a severe issue.

---

[4] See *The Divine Code*, 2nd ed. Pp. 64 – 74.

Although this mode of behavior is in step with the letter of the law, it fails to acknowledge the spirit of the law. It is a liberal approach to Torah law and Noahism.

The Spirit and Letter of the Law: The Shabbat of a Pious Noahide

One, who seeks to go beyond the letter of the law as a matter of piety, will refrain from any observance of Shabbat. A pious, God fearing, religious Noahide will not attempt to observe Shabbat in any way by resting. A Noahide who imitates Jewish observance of Shabbat by "resting" is a less observant Noahide than one who does not observe Shabbat at all!

Observance vs. Acknowledgement

Until now, we have only discussed the *observance* of Shabbat. By *observance*, however, we mean refraining from labor or imitating other Jewish Shabbat obligations. However, this prohibition does not preclude Noahides having a positive, meaningful connection with Shabbat in another way.

At the beginning of creation, Shabbat was established as a day of rest for Hashem (only), but also as a commemoration of the work of creation, a testament that G-d created the world in seven days. According to many, this latter aspect of Shabbat should be acknowledged by all non-Jews.[5] The Midrash says:[6]

> [The wicked Turnus Rufus][7] asked Rabbi Akiva: "From where can you prove to me that God wished to honor the Seventh Day?" … Rabbi Akiva responded: "Verify it with [via necromancy,] because a spirit will ascend on any day of the week except for Shabbat – verify it with the spirit of your father!"… Turnus Rufus checked the veracity of Rabbi Akiva's claim with the spirit of his own father. His father's spirit ascended on every day of the week except Shabbat. On the following Sunday, Turnus Rufus again raised his father and asked him, "father, is it possible that you became a Jew after you died, that you now observe Shabbat? Why did you ascend every day of the week, but did not ascend on Shabbat?" He [Turnus Rufus's father] answered him, saying: "Anyone who does not willingly observe the Sabbath among the living is forced to do so among the dead!"

---

[5] This also appears to be the opinion of the *Mishneh LaMelech, Melachim* 10:7 and *Kli Yakar* to Exodus 20:8. However, the *Maharanach* in his Torah commentary appears to hold that even verbal acknowledgment of Shabbat by non-Jews is prohibited. See *Toldos Noach, Matza Chein* 9:4 for a discussion and comparison of the sources.

[6] *Bereshis Rabbah 11:5.*

[7] The brutal Roman governor of Israel in the times of the Mishnah.

The *Maharzu*[8] explains that the spirit of Turnus Rufus's father could not mean that non-Jews must observe Shabbat. Rather, it means that any non-Jew who denies the significance of Shabbat will be "forced to do so among the dead." What does it mean "forced to do so among the dead?" The Midrash goes on to explain that the wicked are punished with the fires of Gehinnom (purgatory) every day of the week, but are given respite on Shabbat. One who denies the existence and significance of Shabbat, even a Non-Jew, will apparently be held accountable.

Furthermore, Noahide acknowledgement of Shabbat goes back to the beginning of creation. There is a fascinating *Midrash*[9] about Adam, Kayin, and the composition of Psalm 92:

> *Adam met Kayin and asked of him: "What happened? What was your judgment?"*

> *Kayin replied: "I repented and it was mitigated"*

> *Adam began slapping his own face and cried out: "Such is the power of repentance – and I didn't know it!"* *Adam immediately arose and declared:* Mizmor shir le-yom ha-Shabbat, a Psalm, a song for the Shabbos...

Psalm 92, recited by Adam for Shabbat, only mentions Shabbat in its opening. It then goes on to praise God's deeds and creations, curiously contrasting the permanence of His deeds with the temporary follies of the wicked, and then concludes with the praises of the righteous man.

What is the connection between the ideas of *teshuvah*, repentance, the temporary prospering of the wicked, and the Shabbos?

Speaking with Kayin, Adam realized the power of repentance and marveled at its greatness. *Teshuvah* is the great creation for which Adam praises God. God is also praised for His incredible kindness: He does not execute judgment immediately. Rather, He waits, allowing transgressors time to either do *teshuvah* or lose themselves further. Alternatively, Adam also realized that this world is the place of finite recompense. Here a person is rewarded for the minority of his deeds. Therefore, the wicked are often rewarded for their few mitzvos, while the righteous are often punished for their few *aveiros*, sins.

---

[8] Rav Zeev Wolf Einhorn d.1862 – major expounder on the Midrash.

[9] *Bereshis Rabbah* 22.

But what does this all have to do with Shabbos? When God rested on Shabbos, he beheld the goodness of His creation – he saw that it was well suited for its purpose. So too, Adam, in his revelation, suddenly understood the "big picture" – the greatness of God's world and the incredible potential that it offered.

In that revelation, he saw the "big plan" – he understood the nature of reward and punishment, the fate of the wicked, and the ultimate reward of the righteous. He understood his purpose and how the world was designed for it.

Rashi understands this Psalm as, primarily, an acknowledgement of the World to Come, the ultimate Shabbos.

We see that Adam's relationship to Shabbat was not one of rest. It was a relationship to Shabbos as the capstone of creation, the zecher le-maaseh bereshis, the commemoration of G-d's having created the world in seven days. If there is any aspect of Shabbos that is proper to be acknowledged by Noahides, then this is it.

It is therefore appropriate to base the Noahide acknowledgement of Shabbat on Psalm 92 and Adam's epiphany. In this way, Noahides are following in the way of Adam, to whom the Noahide laws were commanded.

THE YESHIVA PIRCHEI SHOSHANIM SHULCHAN ARUCH LEARNING
PROJECT

The Noahide Laws – Lesson Twenty Six

164 Village Path, Lakewood NJ 08701 732.370.3344
164 Rabbi Akiva, Bnei Brak, 03.616.6340

Outline of This Lesson:

1. Introduction: Torah Time

2. The Starting Point: Mishnah Rosh HaShanah 1:2

3. Connecting to the Festivals

4. One Day vs. Two Days

5. Rosh HaShanah: Introduction

6. The New Year?

7. Rosh HaShanah – A Day of Many Meanings

8. Elul – The Month of Preparation

9. Summary

Festivals I: Introduction & Rosh HaShanah

Lesson

26

Introduction: Torah Time

The Torah establishes a spiritual calendar for the world. However, this calendar does not represent a single conception of time. Instead, the spiritual calendar is a complex affair of concentric, interlocking cycles.[1] For example, the Mishnah (_Rosh HaShanah 1:1_) tells us that there are several _Rosh Hashanah's_ (New Years), each demarcating a unique cycle of time. These cycles run concurrently, overlaying each other, creating an ever-shifting mosaic of seasons:

> _There are four_ Rosh Hashanah's _[New Years]: the 1ˢᵗ of Nissan is the New Year for kings and festivals, the 15ᵗʰ of Elul is the New Year for the tithing of animals (according to Rabbis Elazar and Shimon, this is on the 1ˢᵗ of Tishrei), the 1ˢᵗ of Tishrei for counting years, the Jubilee and Shemitta cycles, and the tithing of trees and produce. The 1ˢᵗ of Shvat is the New Year for trees according to the yeshiva [school] of Shammai. According to the yeshiva [school] of Hillel, it is on the 15ᵗʰ of Shvat._

This flow of spiritual time is demarcated by a number of holy days that give it shape and meaning. For most of these holidays, their significance exists on two levels. One level is universal and important to all peoples. The other level is specific and narrowly applicable to Israel alone.

---

[1] The Hebrew calendar acknowledges and integrates a number of astronomical cycles. Contrary to popular belief, the Hebrew calendar is not a lunar calendar. Rather, it is a _lunisolar_ calendar, a calendar based upon both the solar and lunar astronomical cycles. This resolution is necessary to keep the Torah's holidays within their designated seasons, as it is written: "These are festivals of the Lord that you shall proclaim in their appointed seasons." (Lev. 23:4). A purely lunar calendar results in an 11 day per-year drift in the holidays. This drift is the reason why the Islamic holidays, relying upon a purely lunar calendar, occur 11 days earlier each year. Furthermore, there is a larger solar cycle commemorated by _Birkas HaChamma_ (a blessing on the renewal of the sun) every 28 years.

For example, let's look at the holiday of Sukkot. For Israel, it commemorates God's providence and guardianship of Israel via the *ananei ha-Kavod*, clouds of glory, which surrounded Israel as they traveled in the desert.[2]

The festival huts built on this holiday are in commemoration of these clouds.[3] We see that the *mitzvah* of building *sukkot*, huts, is of unique significance to Israel. This is true of many of the Torah's commandments pertaining to Sukkot.

However, Sukkot is also the holiday on which the world is judged for water.[4] This point is of universal significance; water is the life-blood of the world. It is fundamental to the survival of every living thing and to planetary ecology. The amount of rain and its geographic distribution is determined on this holiday. Some may be judged for drought, others for flood. However we pray that each nation and person will receive just the right amount.

Additionally, offerings were given on sukkot to atone for the nations of the world. While the Jews have *Yom Kippur*, the other nations of the world have sukkot.

For Noahides, these aspects of Sukkot are the most relevant. They transcend the specific observances of Israel, addressing common concerns for all of humanity and the world.

As we embark on our study of the Torah's holidays, our goal is to identify which holidays have universal significance, the nature of that significance, and how that significance may be positively expressed by Noahides.

The Starting Point: *Mishnah, Rosh HaShanah* 1:2

At four junctures, the world is judged: on Passover for grain, on Shavuot for fruits, on Rosh Hashanah all pass before him like sheep of the flock, as it is written, "He form their hearts as one, he understands all of their deeds." (Psalms 33). On Sukkot, the world is judged for water.

---

[2] Specifically, Sukkot commemorates the return of the Clouds of Glory. See *Kol Eliyahu* 84. The clouds departed after the sin of the golden calf. It was only after their national atonement and the building of the Tabernacle that the clouds returned. This was on the 15th of Nissan. The specific observances of sukkot are mostly linked to this episode in the history if Israel.

[3] Bottom of *Sukkot* 11b.

[4] *Mishnah, Rosh HaShanah 1:2.*

This Mishnah teaches us which of the Torah's holidays hold universal significance and are important for the entire world. It also tells us the main themes of these holidays.

A BRIEF OVERVIEW OF THE MISHNAH

On Passover for grain... – On Passover God decides upon the volume and distribution of the world's grain production. While the liberation from Egypt, observance of the Passover sacrifices, the *Seder*, etc. are all uniquely Jewish concerns; the concern for worldwide food resources is universal. For Noahides, this is the central concern of the Passover holiday.

On Shavuot for fruits... – On Shavuot the world is judged as to whether the fruit trees will yield enough produce to sustain the world's population. Shavuot is also the commemoration of the giving of the Torah at Sinai. For Noahides, the giving of the Torah holds special significance because it was then that the Noahide laws were reaffirmed by Moses. On Shavuot, the original Noahide covenant was placed under the umbrella of Sinaitic obligation. For Noahides, these are the two central themes of Shavuot: the reaffirmation of the Noahide laws and the judgment on the produce of trees.

On Rosh HaShanah all pass before him like sheep of the flock... – All the peoples of the world are judged according to their deeds on Rosh HaShanah. This includes Noahides as well as Jews. While the blowing of the shofar is unique to the Jews, the general idea of repentance and judgment is important to all. As we shall see, many of the customs of Rosh HaShanah (meaning non-*mitzvah* practices) are reasonable and relevant for Noahides as well.

On Sukkot, the world is judged for water... – The abundance and availability of fresh water (for drinking, rains, rivers, etc.) is determined on the holiday of Sukkot. Additionally, this was the holiday upon which offerings and prayers were given on behalf of the 70 gentile nations. Sukkot therefore has two meanings for Noahides: It is the day upon which Noahides pray for and acknowledge the importance of water, one of the creations of the First Day.[5] It is also the time of atonement for the nations of the world.

---

[5] The creation narrative implies that water existed at the beginning of creation. However, the Midrash explains that it was impossible for anything to have existed prior to creation. The Midrash derives that ten things must have been created on the first day: the heavens and the earth, the *tohu* and *vohu* (void and primeval chaos), light and dark, wind and water, and the time of day and time of night (since the heavenly bodies were not yet created, day and night must have been defined as times instead of the products of planetary motion).

Connecting to the Festivals

Noahides have no obligation to observe any of the Torah's festivals, even those that have universal relevance. Nevertheless, the importance of these festivals for the entire world compels their acknowledgement.

As we have mentioned many times in this course, Noahism has not existed as a living faith in over 1700 years. As a result, any customs, practices, or prayers unique to it have long since vanished. The goal of this project is not to attempt to recreate something that is long since lost, but to define the *halachic* (Torah practice) boundaries of Noahism and establish its parameters so that it can grow and flourish.

Much of what will be brought here are outlines of suggested customs and prayers for these holidays. The Noahide community will, undoubtedly and over time, develop their own liturgy and customs. Until then, these suggestions may serve as a springboard.

One Day Vs. Two Days

Jews outside of Israel observe the Torah festivals for two days instead of one day (the exception, however, is Rosh HaShanah, which is always observed for two days whether in Israel or the Diaspora). An extra day was added to the holidays by the ancient sages due to a unique diaspora problem. At that time the new month was declared based upon the sighting and reporting of the new moon in Israel. Communicating the decree of the new month to the diaspora was fraught with problems. The issues involved often delayed the news of the new month from reaching diaspora settlements. At most, these delays could create a variance of one day in the diaspora calendar. Therefore, the ancient sages decreed that diaspora Jews should add an additional day to alleviate the calendrical doubt.

Nowadays, with our fixed calendar, there is no practical need for a second day. Nevertheless, the Jewish community still keeps this additional day because the original decree that established it was never abolished.

It is not known if the ancient Noahide communities observed or acknowledged the Torah festivals in any way. This fact, combined with the lack of continuity and voluntary nature of Noahide observance, makes it clear that the rabbinic decree of a second day is not relevant to Noahides.

Furthermore, by keeping only the Biblically ordained date of the holiday (as do the Jews in Israel), Noahides are making a positive distinction as to their unique relationship to the holidays.

Rosh HaShanah: Introduction

...on Rosh Hashanah all pass before him like sheep of the flock, as it is written, "He forms their hearts as one, he understands all of their deeds."

...on Rosh Hashanah all pass before him like sheep of the flock,

Rashi comments on this Mishnah in Rosh HaShanah 18a. He explains that when a shepherd counts his sheep for tithes, he lets them pass one-by-one through a small opening into a corral. The opening, being too small for two sheep to pass at once, ensures that they can are counted properly as they pass through. It also gives the shepherd a chance to examine each sheep individually. According to this explanation, each person is responsible for his own judgment; it is between him and his "shepherd." Furthermore, Rosh Hashanah is a passage through a "narrow place." It is a day upon which all things hang in the balance. However,

"He forms their hearts as one, he understands all of their deeds."

This verse is surprising, because it appears to contradict what we just learned! If Rosh HaShanah is a time of individual judgment, then why does this verse imply that it is a time of communal judgment? The Talmud explains that this verse means that on Rosh HaShanah God also sees the hearts of all mankind in a single glance.

The correct way to read this Mishnah, then, is that it is teaching us two things. One is that Rosh Hashanah is the time when one must face his creator as an individual, taking sole responsibility for his actions and being. The other, is that on Rosh Hashanah mankind and all its deeds is viewed as a whole. On Rosh Hashanah, God judges human society in all of its complexity and the vast network of interpersonal relationships therein.

The New Year?

As we mentioned above, spiritual time is a complicated motion of wheels-within-wheels. The Mishnah tells us that there are a number of years running concurrently, each with their own Rosh HaShanah:

There are four Rosh Hashanah's [New Years]: the 1ˢᵗ of Nissan is the New Year for kings and festivals, the 15ᵗʰ of Elul is the New Year for the tithing of animals (according to Rabbis Elazar and Shimon, this is on the 1ˢᵗ of Tishrei), the 1ˢᵗ of Tishrei for counting years, the Jubilee and Shemitta cycles, and the tithing of trees and produce.

The 1ˢᵗ of Shvat is the New Year for trees according to the yeshiva [school] of Shammai. According to the yeshiva [school] of Hillel, it is on the 15ᵗʰ of Shvat.

The Rosh HaShanah of the 1ˢᵗ of Tishrei is the BIG Rosh HaShanah. This is the Rosh HaShanah that determines how we actually count our years. However, the month of Tishrei is not the first month. The first month is actually Nissan.

It seems counter-intuitive to count years starting in the middle of the cycle of months. However, it makes sense when you think of the "year" as a number of years occurring at the same time. The first day of the first month, the month of Nissan, is the Rosh HaShanah for kings and festivals. This year deals with counting the reign of kings, dating of legal documents, and the cycle of festival offerings in the temple.

The BIG Rosh HaShanah, however, is concerned with the spiritual relationship between man and his creator. While months are counted according to the civil calendar, the BIG picture – years – is determined according to the spiritual cycle.

This point is reinforced by a fascinating dispute in the Talmud Rosh HaShanah 10b – 11a:

- Rabbi Eliezer offers evidence to prove that creation occurred in Tishrei (the seventh month).

- Rabbi Yehoshua offers evidence that creation happened in Nissan (the first month).

Rabbeinu Tam[6] points out that they are not actually arguing. There were actually two creations. The first, in Tishrei, was the creation of the world in thought. This was the purer, spiritual, creation of the world in abstract. The creation of Nissan, however, was the physical creation of the world. The *Mases Binyamin* notes[7] that this explains many differences between the year that beings in Nissan and the year that begins in Tishrei.

We count years according to the very beginning of God's thought: Tishrei. In doing so, we assign greater importance to the abstract, prime spiritual creation rather than the physical creation of Nissan.

---

[6] Tosafos Rosh HaShanah 27a.

[7] In Shu"t 101. He points out that we calculate years based on the assumption that the world was created in Tishrei. However, many other astronomical calculations are based on the assumption that the world was created in Nissan.

Rosh Hashanah: a Day of Many Meanings

When Rabbi Eliezer tells us that the creation occurred in Tishrei, he means that the creation was completed in Tishrei on the first day of the month. The creation actually began on the 25th day of Elul, culminating with the creation of Adam on the final sixth day of creation.

Rosh Hashanah is, more properly, the birthday of Adam and the anniversary of the creation of man. However, the joy of this event is dampened by the fact that it is also the anniversary of Adam and Eve's fall.

Because Rosh HaShanah commemorates two events of opposing natures, it is a holiday full of paradoxical meanings. It is a day of celebration, yet also of judgment and trepidation. It is a day of joy, yet solemnity. It is also a time of great mercy, as well as great severity.

The preparation, prayers, and customs of Rosh Hashanah all acknowledge this subtle weave of meanings.

Rosh Hashanah is ultimately a time of renewal. It is the day when each person must search his deeds, evaluating his relationships both with God and his fellow men, righting wrongs and starting anew.

Elul – A Month of Preparation

Preparations for Rosh Hashanah actually begin a month before the holiday, starting on the first of Elul. Since ancient times, the month of Elul has been a time of introspection and review. It was on the first of this month that Moses ascended Sinai to beseech forgiveness for the Jewish people. It is also during this month that creation began.

Starting on the first of Elul, every person should devote time daily to consider his relationship with God, his neighbors, and his family. A person should assess who he is now, who he wants to be, and how to attain these goals.

Our goal in the month of Elul is change; we set out to change who we are, to show God that we can be different, better people. In English, this process is called repentance. In Hebrew the term is *teshuvah*.

Teshuvah: Technical vs. Colloquial Use

Colloquially, the term *teshuvah* is employed to mean any type of repentance. However, *Teshuva* also has very specific, technical meanings. In the course of your studies you may come across the statement: "There is no *teshuvah* for Non-Jews,[8]" or "There is no *teshuvah* for Noahides." When you see this statement, remember that it is dealing with the technical definition of *teshuvah*, which is far more complicated than the way the word is commonly used. The technical definition of *teshuvah* is only relevant to Jews. However, there are other types of repentance. For example, many explain that the type of repentance relevant to Noahides is called *charata*. The details of these technical distinctions, however, are entirely theoretical and have little-to-no practical impact on Noahide practice. There is certainly repentance for Noahides regardless of whether the technical term for that repentance is *teshuvah*, *charata*, or anything else. After all, the story of Jonah is all about non-Jewish repentance.[9]

ACTION:

PSALM 27

The custom of Jews, starting on the first day of Elul, is to recite Psalm 27 daily, both in the morning and evening (around sunset or at night). The Midrash explains that this psalm contains a number of subtle references to the period of repentance and the holidays. It is certainly appropriate for Noahides to recite this psalm as part of their preparations for Rosh Hashanah. This twice-daily recitation of Psalm 27 continues from the 1st of Elul through the 21st of Tishrei.[10]

Psalm 27

To be recited in the morning and at sunset (or at night), daily, from the 1st of Elul to the 21st of Tishrei. Commentary is found in the footnotes.

Of David: the Lord is my light[11] and my salvation.[12] Of whom shall I be afraid? The Lord is the strength of my life. Of whom shall I dread? When evil-doers – my

---

[8] See *Midrash Tanchuma*, Haazinu 4.

[9] Resolving *Midrash Tanchumah* against *Sefer Yonah* has elicited much discussion among the Acharonim. See *Sefer Ratz KeTzvi: Yerach HaEisanim* 13 for an extensive discussion of the issues.

[10] This, as we shall see, is the period of the holidays for Noahides and Jews.

[11] The Midrash understands this as a reference to Rosh Hashanah.

[12] The salvation mentioned here is the atonement of the holiday season. For Jews it refers to the atonement of Yom Kippur, for Noahides the atonement of Sukkot.

tormentors and opponents[13] – draw near to devour my flesh, it is they who stumble and fall. Though an army may besiege me, my heart will not fear. Should warfare arise against me, in this alone I shall trust.[14]

I have asked one thing of the Lord, only this have I sought: that I may dwell in the house of the Lord all the days of my life, to behold the pleasantness of the Lord, and to meditate within His sanctuary.[15]

On the day of evil He will hide me within His shelter. He will conceal me in the innermost shelter of his tent. He will lift me up upon a rock. And now he will raise my head above my foes who surround me. I will slaughter in his tent joyous offerings. I will sing and make music to the Lord. Lord, hear my voice when I call! Favor me and answer me! For your sake has my heart spoke to me: "Seek his presence!" O God, I seek your presence! Do not conceal your countenance from me! Do not repel your servant in anger! You have been my help. Do not forsake me, do not abandon me, O God of my salvation!

Though my father and mother have abandoned me,[16] the Lord shall gather me in. Teach me your way, O Lord, and on account of my watchful foes[17] set me upon a straight path. Do not give me over to their wishes for they have set against me false witnesses who breathe violence.

---

[13] The evil-doers and opponents mentioned in this psalm are primarily internal. They are the devices of the *yetzer ha-ra*, the evil inclination. They are also the memories and emotions associated with one's past misdeeds. These memories often torment a person and hamper their ability to return to God. This will be discussed more in a future lesson.

[14] Rashi and Radak explain that this refers to the opening line "The Lord is my light and my salvation," which is the process of Rosh HaShanah and subsequent atonement. One must trust in this process. Once a person has returned to God and reestablished a positive relationship with God, then God will protect and shelter him. Alternatively, Ibn Ezra explains that this phrase refers to the next sentence: *I have asked one thing of the Lord, only this have I sought: that I may dwell in the house of the Lord all the days of my life...* One should trust in God because he (the penitent) ultimately desires spiritual success and not the vain achievements of this world.

[15] Writes the *Malbim*, that despite the many desires and needs a person may have, the desire to know his creator is the ultimate, all inclusive desire of the soul.

[16] Sforno explains that once a person becomes an adult he must find his own way in the world. He can no longer rely upon his parents to make choices for him. He must choose his values and make his own decisions. Although his parents are no longer his guiding voice, the Lord is always there. God is eternally our father and guide.

[17] The Hebrew here is a little difficult to translate. The word for "Watchful foes" is related to the word for "staring" or "gazing." In the context of our verse, it refers to those who stare maliciously. The psalm is asking God to frustrate the wishes of those who maliciously watch and mock one who wishes to come back to God. See Radak.

Had I not believed[18] that I would see the goodness of the Lord in the land of life![19] Hope to the Lord! Be strong and He will give you courage[20] – and hope to the Lord!

Studying For Elul: Works on Repentance

In Elul, many prepare by studying works of *mussar* (personal development) or writings on *Teshuva* (repentance). There are, thank God, many, many books addressing these topics. The following are a few suggested titles:

- *Returnity*, by R' Tal Zwecker

- *The Power of Teshuvah*, by R' Heshy Kleinman

- *A Touch of Purity*, by R' Yechiel Spero

- *Teshuvah, Restoring Life*, by R' Reuven Leuchter

- *Teshuvah*, by S. Felbrand

- *Thirty Days to Teshuva*, by R' Zvi Miller

- *Crown Him With Joy*, by R' Hadar Margolin

- *Gates of Repentance*, by Rabbeinu Yonah

During Elul, many are accustomed to study and use the advice given by Rabbeinu Yonah in his *Gates of Repentance*, in a section called *The Foundation of Repentance* (the full text of *Gates of Repentance* is available in translation from Feldheim Publishers.) We have provided a translation of this section here:

---

[18] Rashi explains: Were it not for my faith in God, my enemies would have destroyed me and I would have never merited to achieve closeness to God.

[19] Meaning the World to Come. See *Brachos* 4a.

[20] Strength in faith is the ultimate source of all courage.

Gate of Repentance: The Foundation of Repentance
by Rabbeinu Yonah of Gerona c. 1250 CE

The Holy One, blessed is He, taught us through his servants, the prophets, and [specifically] through Yechezkel the prophet [Yechezkel 18:30-31]:

Repent, and cause others to repent, from all your transgressions so that they shall not be a stumbling block of iniquity for you. Cast away from yourselves all your transgressions and make for yourselves a new heart and a new spirit. Why should you die?

You, who have transgressed and sinned, and now comes to seek refuge under the wings of the Divine Presence, to enter into the ways of repentance, I shall instruct you and enlighten you in the path to travel.

On that day,[21] you shall cast away all the sins that you have committed and consider yourself as if you were born today; as if you have neither merit nor fault. This day is the beginning of your deeds. Starting today, you shall weigh all your actions in order that your steps not veer from the good path. This path will bring you to repentance, a complete return, because it is as if you have cast from your shoulders the heaviness of all the transgressions you have committed. Thus your thoughts will neither haunt nor confuse you nor prevent you from repenting because of embarrassment from your sins. This is because [otherwise] your thoughts will say to you: "How could I be so brazen to repent after I have sinned and transgressed, doing such-and-such over and over? How could I raise my face before Him? [I am] like a thief who has been caught - I am too embarrassed to stand before Him! And how can I show myself in his courtyard, how could I keep his laws?"

Do not think like this! The evil inclination sits like a fly in the chambers of the heart, renewing himself every day, watching and waiting to make you stumble. He puts these destructive thoughts in your heart. Instead, you should remember that this is the nature of the Creator, may He be blessed: that His hand is outstretched to receive the penitent. Therefore, it is good for you to cast off your sins and make for yourself a new heart.

And so shall you do on the day that you decide to return: When your spirit moves you to become a servant of your Creator, you shall offer up your prayer before Him and say:

"Please God, I have sinned and transgressed, (and such and such I did...) from the day I came upon the Earth until this very day. And now, my heart has moved me and my spirit has pressed me to return to You in

---

[21] Meaning the day one decides to return to God.

truth and with a good and complete heart – with all my heart, soul, and all that is dear to me – and to admit and cast aside my ways; to cast away from myself all my sins and to make for myself a new heart and a new spirit, and to be meticulous and careful in my fear of You. And You, Lord, my God, who opens His hand with repentance, helping those who come to purify themselves, open Your hand and receive me with complete repentance before You. Help me to strengthen myself in fear of You. Help me against the evil inclination, who wages war against me with cunning strategies, seeking to entrap my soul and destroy men, that it should not rule over me. Distance it from my 248 limbs and cast it into the depths of the sea. Thwart it so that it shall not stand at my right side to accuse me.[22] Help me so that I shall go in Your laws. Remove from me this heart of stone and grant me a heart of flesh.

Please O Lord, my God, listen to the prayer of Your servant and to his supplications and receive my return unto You. Do not let any sin prevent my prayer and return. May there come before Your holy throne upright defenders to defend me and bring my prayer before You. And if, on account of my many and great sins, there is no one to defend me, then make an opening from under Your throne of glory and receive my repentance so that I should not return empty from before You; for only you listen to prayer."

You should habituate yourself to always say this prayer.

And such is the path that you should walk and the actions to which you should accustom yourself so that you will be on guard from all sin. In the morning, when you wake from your sleep, you should think in your mind that you will repent and examine your ways. You should strive, in accordance with your ability, not to stray.

At meal-times, before you eat, you should confess your sins. If you strayed in anything, you should confess it. This confession will distance you from all sin and transgression. Because, if a sin comes your way, you will be cautious of it and say in your heart: "How could I do this great, evil thing and then confess on it later? Why, I would be of those of which it is said, [*Tehillim* 78:36] 'Nevertheless they did flatter him with their mouth, and they lied unto him with their tongues. For their heart was not right with him, neither were they steadfast in his covenant.' I would be like one who immerses [in a *mikveh*] while holding an impure creature! I would be foolish and with little intellect before my Creator for not having being able to stand up to my lusts even for a short time like this!"

---

[22] One's own evil inclination stands against Him as prosecutor.

And when you put this to your heart and spirit, you will then be guarded from sin.
.

You should be swift as a deer and strong as a lion to do the will of your father in heaven. This applies even to minor things because all your ways will be measured. And so King David said [*Tehillim* 49:6]:

> *Why should I fear in the days of evil, when the iniquity of my heels shall compass me about.*

This verse speaks of the sins and *mitzvot* that men trample with their heels (meaning sins that most people are not careful about) and consider them to be nothing.

When the time to eat comes, and you search yourself and find nothing, then you should thank and praise the Creator who has helped you against your enemies, and that you merited to have one hour of *teshuva* in this world. Like this you should then eat your meal. Afterwards, when the evening meal comes, you should confess beforehand everything, as I have said. And so you should do from the time of eating your evening meal until the time to sleep [meaning, a third confession before sleep].

We have, therefore, three daily opportunities for this confession. Thus should you do every day from the first day of your *teshuva* and afterwards, for one month or one year, until you are strengthened in the fear of the Creator and have succeeded in abandoning your bad habits.

And when you can guard yourself from the sins to which you were habituated, finding that you had many opportunities to transgress yet did not do so, you should no longer fear. From heaven you were helped… And regarding the previous sins that you had cast off from yourself, you should be always regretful and seek from God to erase them from the heavenly record. You should also chastise your soul over them. If you are of delicate constitution, and cannot tolerate difficult chastisement and fasts, you should at least restrict your desires, in particular those for food and drink.

So said said the pious Rabbi Avraham bar Dovid, "the best safeguard, the greatest and best, is to refrain from over-indulging in food." He explained his words, saying that this is not to mean that one should refrain altogether from eating meat and drinking wine. After all, what has already been forbidden is enough. Rather, he means that while you are eating and still desire to eat more, you should stop in honor of your Creator, and not eat according to your whole desire. This practice will save you from sin and remind you of the love of the Creator more than fasting once a week. That is because this practice is every day, always, when you eat or drinks – then you should refrain from your desire for the honor of your Creator.

You should put your heart to the Torah. If you were accustomed to learning one page each day, then you should learn two. This is because Torah study leads to action. And you should subjugate yourself, forcing your innate desires to be for Torah and the fulfillment of *mitzvos*…

You should not be haphazard in your service of the Creator. Rather you should serve Him with a complete heart. You should never neglect any matter because of laziness or embarrassment…

Even if the world mocks you, nevertheless you should be like a simpleton in their eyes rather than transgress even a small *mitzva* of the Creator's *mitzvos*. Regarding this it is written "in its love you shall be ravished always" (Mishlei 5:19), which means - for the love of a *mitzva*, you should be ravished and simple to leave all things and to work on it. We have found an example of this by Rebbi Elazar ben Pedas, who would sit in the lower market of Tzipori and toil in Torah while his cloak lay in the upper market of the town. He appeared like a simpleton in the eyes of the world because of his love of *mitzvos* and of the Creator [Talmud *Eruvin* 54b]. And if one does this and dies at half of his days, he is given reward as if he had lived all 70 years. This is what King Shlomo said in his wisdom [*Koheles* 5:11]:

> *The sleep of the working man is pleasant, whether he eats little or much.*

This means that whether one's days are many or few, the reward for the few is like the reward for the many.

Moshe toiled for the Jewish people 40 years, and Shmuel HaNavi only ten years, nevertheless the verse equates both of them as one, as it is written [*Tehillim* 99:6]:

> *Moshe and Aaron among his priests, and Shmuel among them that call upon his name.*

The penitent should not muse to himself and say: "Why should I toil in vain? I will waste my strength for nothing! How can my repentance stand against my sins? All that I am capable of doing will not help against all the sins that I have done!"

Don't say this. The Holy One, blessed is He, promised through the prophet Yechezkel that one's sins will not be recalled again, as it is written [*Yechezkel* 18:21-22]:

> *But if the wicked will turn from all his sins that he has committed, and keep all my statutes, and do that which is lawful and right, he shall surely live, he shall not die. All his transgressions that he has committed, they shall not be mentioned to him; in his righteousness that he has done he shall live.*

And there are many more verses for those haunted by their sins, to strengthen them to repent as is written [*Yechezkel* 33:10-11]:

> *Say to them, By My life, says the L-rd, I desire not the death of the wicked, but that the wicked turn from his way, and live. Repent, repent from your evil ways; why should you die, O children of Israel?*

And through all his servants, the prophets, He warned us many times on the matter of *teshuva*. And also our teachers, the Sages of the generations, warned us very much on *teshuva* saying "repent one day before your death" [*Pirkei Avot*].

And they said, "the level of the one who has repented is greater than that of the completely righteous." This is what they meant when they said "in the place where the penitent stands, the perfectly righteous does not stand" [Repentance] is one of the things created before the creation of the world. Likewise they said in the *Midrash Bereishis* [4:13] "*And Kayin said to God, 'is my sin too great to bear?'* - he repented."
Therefore this verse has 7 words, (hinting) that repentance rises up until the holy throne, the 7 firmaments, 7 realms…

Therefore, every God fearing person should put in his heart the fear of the Creator and repent from all his sins. He should prepare for himself a new, clean, pure heart with which to serve his Creator. He should accustom himself to all that has been written. He should use his intelligence to think of ways in which he could fear the Lord, the Great and Awesome One, and engage such matters between him privately, away from the eyes of men.

Fortunate is one who merits and causes others to merit. The entire world was created for such a person, as it is written [*Koheles* 12:13]:

The end of the matter, all having been heard, is fear God and keep his mitzvos, *for this is the sum of man."*

Our sages have expounded this verse to mean [Talmud *Berachos* 6] "The entire world was created as a companion for such a person."

The Noahide Laws – Lesson Twenty Seven

Outline of This Lesson:

1. Introduction

2. When To Start Saying *Selichos*

3. The Custom Noahides Should Follow

4. In Practice

5. Action Point

6. Structure of *Selichos*

7. Suggested *Selichos* Service

Festivals II: Selichos

Lesson

27

Introduction

The second phase Rosh HaShanah preparation is the recitation of *Selichos* – penitential prayers. These prayers are meant to prepare the soul for Rosh HaShanah. Since Rosh HaShanah is the day upon which the heart of every person (Jew and Noahide alike) is examined, it makes sense that every person should prepare. The recitation of *Selichos* is thus appropriate for both Jews and Noahides.

When to Start Saying *Selichos*?

Selichos are usually said in the early, pre-dawn, hours and followed by one's regular devotions. As with all Noahide prayers, there is no quorum required for their recitation. They may be said by an individual or by a group of people. There are two different customs as to when to begin saying *Selichos*.

The Sephardi Custom According to the Sephardi custom (the custom of the Jews of Spain, North Africa, and the Middle East), *Selichos* are said for the entire month of Elul. The reason for this is that Moses ascended Sinai on the first of Elul and remained there all month. He spent the time petitioning for his people and, eventually, received the second set of tablets. Selichos are recited for the entire month in commemoration and imitation of Moses's petitioning upon Sinai.

The Ashkenazi Custom Ashkenazi custom (the custom of the Jews of Europe and most of America) is a little more complicated. The Ashkenazi custom has two requirements. First, is that there must be a minimum of four days of *Selichos* before Rosh HaShanah. Second, is that *Selichos* must start after the preceding Shabbat. Therefore, if Rosh

HaShanah starts on a Wednesday night, then *Selichos* start after the preceding Shabbat. However, if Rosh HaShanah starts on a Monday night, then *Selichos* starts after the Shabbat preceding the Shabbat before Rosh Hashanah. In such a case, *Selichos* are said for almost 10 days.

This custom has a fascinating source. In the Torah's list of the festival offerings[1] it states over and over: "You shall bring…" However, the offering of Rosh HaShanah says: "You shall make…" The sages have noted this subtle difference. On Rosh HaShanah, they explain, a person must make himself like an offering, a sacrifice, to God. He must prepare his soul in the same way in which a sacrifice is prepared for the Temple. Just as a sacrifice must be examined and watched for four days to ensure it is free of a disqualifying blemish, so too must a person search and examine his soul for at least four days prior to Rosh HaShanah.

What is the reason for always beginning after Shabbat? Beginning after Shabbat was originally a practical matter of synagogue logistics. Over time it became standard convention.

Which Custom Should Noahides Follow if They Wish to Say Selichos?

It seems more appropriate for Noahides to follow the Ashkenaz custom with some slight modifications. There are many, many reasons why the Ashkenaz custom is preferable for Noahides. Namely:

1) Moses's ascending Sinai in Elul, the basis for the Sephardic custom, was about seeking atonement for the Jewish sin of the golden calf. This is less relevant to Noahides than the reason behind the Ashkenaz custom. Noahides, after all, have a share in the laws of offerings. In fact, a Noahide may, even today, offer certain sacrifices (something even a Jew cannot do!)

2) Almost all of the texts of the *Selichos* are inapplicable to Noahides. There are barely enough texts for the Ashkenaz custom and certainly not enough to fill out an entire month of *Selichos* according to the Sephardic custom.

---

[1] Numbers, Chapters 28 & 29.

IN PRACTICE

Since the Ashkenaz custom of starting *Selichos* after Shabbat began as a matter of synagogue logistics, it is not relevant to Noahides. For this reason, we suggest that Noahides say *Selichos* only in the four days before Rosh HaShanah. While Jews do not say *Selichos* on Shabbat, the reasons for this omission do not apply to Noahides. Therefore, Noahides who wish to say *Selichos* should began four days before Rosh HaShanah and say them for each of the four days. In 2015 Noahides will say Selichos as follows:

- Thursday, September 10, 2015 – First day of *Selichos* for Noahides. Jews will begin saying *Selichos* on the night of September 5.
- Friday, September 11, 2015 – Second day of *Selichos* for Noahides.
- Saturday, September 12, 2015 – Third day of *Selichos* for Noahides.
- Sunday, September 13, 2015 – Fourth and final day of *Selichos*. Rosh HaShanah begins at night.
- Monday, September 14 – Rosh HaShanah day.

ACTION POINT

There are very, very few existing *Selichos* texts that work for Noahides. The composition of uniquely Noahide *Selichos* is worthwhile and certainly needed for those who wish to say *Selichos*. An excellent source for the format and style of the *Selichos* is The Complete Artscroll Selichos. In the suggested Noahide service below, we have used Psalms associated with the themes of repentance as *Selichos* texts. However, these may certainly be changed out in favor of uniquely Noahide texts.

The Structure of *Selichos*

The *Selichos* service consists of fixed prayers interspersed with the *Selichos* texts. The *Selichos* texts change daily, while the fixed portions remain the same. The outline is as follows:

- Opening Prayers - The *Selichos* service consists of fixed opening prayers.

- *Selichos* - Each *Selicha* (the singular of *Selichos*) is separated by a repeated prayer refrain.

- The Litany – Following *Selichos* we recite a confession.

- Supplication – The concluding prayer.

The following is a suggested *Selichos* service for Noahides. It is adapted from the traditional Ashkenaz *Selichos* service.

Selichos

The First Day

Selichos may be said alone or with a congregation. This service is drafted for a congregation. An individual praying alone should say "I" instead of "we" and "my" instead of "our." An individual also omits congregational responses.

Opening Prayers

Sanctification

Leader: May His great name be ever exalted and sanctified (**Cong.**: Amen!) in the world that He created according to His will. May His kingship reign in our lifetimes and in our days, swiftly and soon, and we say: Amen!

Cong.: Amen! May His great Name be blessed forever and ever!

Leader: May His great name be blessed forever and ever. Blessed, praised, glorified, exalted, extolled, mighty, upraised, and lauded is the name of the Holy One, Blessed is He (**Cong.**: Blessed is He!) exceedingly beyond any blessing and song or praise and consolation that may be uttered in the world, and we say: Amen (**Cong.**:. Amen!)

All continue individually:

To you, Lord, is the righteousness...

To you, Lord, is the righteousness and to us the shamefacedness. What can we plead? What can we say? What can be uttered? How can we justify ourselves? We will search our ways, inspect them, and then we shall return to you, for Your right hand is outstretched to accept those who return. Neither with kindnesses nor worthy deeds do we come before You. Rather, like the poor and needy do we knock upon Your doors. We knock upon your doors, O Merciful and Compassionate One! Please, do not turn us away from You unanswered! Our King, do not turn us away from You unanswered, for You alone hear prayer!

All flesh shall come to You...

All flesh shall come to You, the One who hears prayer. All flesh shall come to bow before You, O Lord. They will come and bow before you, my Lord, and will render honor unto Your name. Come! Let us prostrate ourselves and bow! Let us kneel before God, our maker. Let us come to His dwelling places, let us prostrate at His footstool. Enter His gates with thanksgiving and His courts with praise. Give thanks to Him and praise His name! Exalt the Lord, our God, and bow at His footstool for He is Holy. Exalt the Lord, our God, and bow at His holy mountain for holy is the Lord, our God. Prostrate yourselves before the Lord in His most holy place. Tremble before Him, all who are upon earth.

As for us, through Your abundant kindness we shall enter Your house. We shall prostrate ourselves toward Your holy sanctuary in awe of You. We will bow towards Your holy sanctuary and give thanks to Your name, for Your kindness and truth, because You have exalted Your promise beyond Your name. Come! Let us sing to the *Lord*, let us call out unto the Rock of our salvation! Let us greet Him with thanksgiving, let us call out to Him with praiseful songs. Let us share together in sweet counsel, let us walk in throngs within the house of God.

God is dreaded in the hidden-most counsel of the holy ones, inspiring awe upon all those who surround him. Lift your hands in the sanctuary and bless the Lord. Behold! Bless the Lord, all you servants of the Lord, who stand in the house of the Lord in the nights. For what force is there in heaven or earth comparable to Your deeds and power? For His is the sea and He perfected the dry land; His hands fashioned it. For in His power are the hidden mysteries of the earth; the mountain summits belong to Him. For the soul of every living thing is His – so too is the spirit of all human flesh. Heaven will gratefully praise Your wonders, O Lord. Your faithfulness [will be praised] in the assembly of holy ones. Your arm is great with power. You strengthen Your hand; You exalt Your right hand! The heavens are Yours and the earth too, the earth and its fullness, is yours for you founded them. You shattered the sea with your might; you smashed the heads of sea serpents upon the waters. You established order upon the earth; summer and winter – you fashioned them. You crushed the heads of the leviathan and You served it as food to the nation of legions. You split open fountain and stream, You dried the mighty rivers. The day is Yours and the night, as well, is Yours. You established luminaries and the sun – You, who performs great deeds that are beyond comprehension and wonders without number. For the Lord is a great God, a great king who is above all heavenly powers. For You are great and work wonders – You alone, O God. For Your kindness is exalted above the very heavens and Your truth is until the upper heavens. The Lord is great and exceedingly lauded. He is awesome above all heavenly powers. Yours, Lord, is the greatness, strength, splendor, triumph, and glory – even everything in heaven and earth! Yours, Lord, is the dominion and sovereignty over every leader. Who could not revere You, O King of the Nations, for in all their kingdom there is none like You. There is none like You, O Lord, for You are great and Your name is great with power. O Lord, God of legions, who is like you, O Strong One, O God? Your faithfulness surrounds you! O Lord, Master of Legions, enthroned above the Cherubim, You alone are God.

Who can express the mighty acts of the Lord, who can announce all His praises? For what in the sky is comparable to the Lord, that can be likened to Him among the angels? What can we say before You who dwells on high? What can we say to You who abides in the highest heaven? What can we say before You, Lord, our God? What can we declare? What justification can we offer? We have no mouth with which to respond. Neither are we so brazen as to raise our heads, for our iniquities are too numerous to count and our sins too vast to be numbered. For

Your Name's sake, O Lord, revive us and, with your righteousness, remove our souls from distress. It is Your way, our God, to delay Your anger against people, both evil and good, and for this You are praised. Act for Your sake, our God, and not for ours. Behold our condition – destitute and empty-handed. The soul is Yours and the body is Your handiwork; take pity on Your labor. **(All continue to the end, but The Leader concludes by reading the following sentences aloud:)** The soul is Yours and the body is Yours. O Lord, act for Your name's sake! We have come, relying upon Your name, O Lord. Act for Your name's sake and because of Your name's glory – for "gracious and merciful God" is Your name! For your name's sake, Lord, may You forgive our iniquity, abundant as it may be.

Cong. first aloud, then repeated aloud by Leader: Forgive us, our father, for in our abundant folly we have erred. Pardon us our King, for our iniquities are many.

Selicha – Psalm 32

The Selicha *texts are poetic creations of the* paytanim *– ancient poets who were masters of the Hebrew language and Jewish liturgy. Their creations deal extensively with the experience of Israel in exile and the restoration of the unique relationship between Israel and God. Due to their specificity, the* Selichos *texts are mostly inapplicable to Noahides. As of today, there are no uniquely Noahide* Selichos. *For this service, we have used Psalms associated with repentance as* Selicha *texts. In the future, Noahides may compose their own unique poems to use in their place.*

All recite Psalm 32 to themselves. The Leader, however, reads the last verse out loud.

Oh God, King, Who sites upon the throne of mercy...

Standing, all recite:
Oh God, King, Who sites upon the throne of mercy, who acts with kindness, forgives iniquities, removes sin, and grants abundant pardon to careless transgressors and forgiveness to rebels – He Who deals righteously with every living being. You do not repay them according to their evil.

Leader: Please do not regard as sinful that which we have done foolishly and transgressed.

Cong.: We have erred, our Rock! Forgive us, O One who has formed us!

The following four verses are recited responsively. Each verse is recited first by the Leader followed by the Congregation:

Hear our voice...

Hear our voice, O Lord, our God, show us pity and compassion, and accept our prayer with compassion and favor.

Bring us back to You Lord, and we will return to you.

Do not cast us away from You, and do not remove Your holy spirit from us.

Do not cast us away in old age; do not forsake us when our strength is exhausted.

All continue individually:

Do not forsake us O Lord, our God, be not distant from us. Display for us a sign for good, so that our enemies may see it and be ashamed, for You, O Lord, will have helped and consoled us. To our sayings give ear, O Lord, perceive our thoughts. May the expressions of our mouth and the thoughts of our heart find favor before You, Lord, our Rock and our Redeemer. Because for You, O Lord, we have waited; You will answer, my Lord, our God.

Confession

All continue individually:
Our God, may our prayer come before You. Do not ignore our supplication, for we are not so brazen and obstinate as to say before You, Lord, our God, that we are righteous and have not sinned, for in truth we have sinned.

The confession is recited with head and body slightly bowed. Strike the left side of the chest with the right first at each bolded word.

WE have **become guilty**, we have **betrayed**, we have **robbed**, we have **spoken slander**, we have **caused perversion**, we have **caused wickedness**, we have **sinned willfully**, we have **extorted,** we have **accused falsely**, we have **given evil counsel**, we have **been deceitful**, we have **scorned**, we have **rebelled**, we have **provoked**, we have **turned away**, we have **been perverse**, we have **acted wantonly**, we have **persecuted**, we have **been obstinate**, we have **been wicked**, we have **corrupted**, we have **been abominable**, we have **strayed**, and You have let us go astray.

We have turned away from Your commandments and from Your good laws but to no avail. Yet, You are righteous in all that has come upon us, for You have acted truthfully while we have caused wickedness.

We have acted wickedly and sinned willfully. Inspire our hearts to abandon the path of evil, as it is written by Your prophet: May the wicked one abandon his way and the vicious man his thoughts; may he return to the Lord and He will show him mercy - to our God, for He is abundantly forgiving.

Your righteous anointed one [David] said before You: "Who can discern mistakes? From unperceived faults cleanse me." Cleanse us Lord, our God, of all our willful sins and purify us, of all our contaminations. Sprinkle upon us pure water and purify us, as it is written by Your prophet: I shall sprinkle pure water upon you and purify you; I will purify you of all your contaminations and of all your abominations.

Micah, your servant, said before You: "Who O God is like You, who pardons iniquity and overlooks transgression for the remnant of his heritage? He who has not retained His wrath eternally, for he desires kindness! He will again be merciful to us; He will suppress our iniquities and cast all sins into the depths of the sea."

Daniel, the greatly beloved man, cried out before You: "Incline Your ear, my God, and listen; open Your eyes and see our desolation and that of the city upon which Your Name is proclaimed. Not because of our righteousness do we cast our supplications before you, but rather because of your abundant compassion. O my Lord, heed! O my Lord, forgive! O my Lord, be attentive and act! Do not delay, for your sake my God, for your Name is proclaimed upon Your city and Your people."

Ezra the scribe said before You: My God, I am embarrassed and ashamed to lift my face to You, for our iniquities have multiplied and our sins have extended unto heaven. You are the God of forgiveness, compassionate and merciful, slow to anger, and abundant in kindness. You have not forsaken us.

Do not forsake us, our Father, do not cast us off, our Creator, do not abandon us, our Molder, and do not bring about our destruction.

Act for the sake...

Act for the sake of Your truth, act for the sake of Your covenant, act for the sake of Your greatness and splendor, act for the sake of Your law, act for the sake of Your glory, act for the sake of Your meeting house, act for the sake of Your remembrance, act for the sake of Your kindness, act for the sake of Your goodness, act for the sake of Your oneness, act for the sake of Your honor, act for the sake of Your teaching, act for the sake of Your kingship, act for the sake of Your eternality, act for the sake of Your counsel, act for the sake of Your power, act for the sake of Your beauty, act for the sake of Your righteousness, act for the sake of Your sanctity, act for the sake of Your abundant mercy, act for the sake of Your presence, act for the sake of Your praise, act for the sake of Your beloved ones who rest in the dust, act for the sake of the desolation of your temple, act for the sake of the ruins of your altar, act for the sake of the martyrs for your holy name; act for the sake of those slaughtered for your oneness, act for the sake of those who entered fire and water for the sanctification of your name, act for the nursing infants who did not err act for the sake of the weaned babes who did not sin, act for the sake of the children at the schoolroom. Act for your sake, if not for ours. Act for your sake and save us!

Answer us...
Answer us, Lord, answer us.
Answer us, Our God, answer us.
Answer us, Our Father, answer us.
Answer us, Our Creator, answer us.
Answer us, Our Redeemer, answer us.
Answer us, He Who Searches Us Out, answer us.
Answer us, Faithful God, answer us.
Answer us, Steadfast and Kind One, answer us.
Answer us, Pure and Upright One, answer us.
Answer us, Living and Enduring One, answer us.
Answer us, Good and Beneficent One, answer us.
Answer us, You Who Knows Inclination, answer us.
Answer us, You Who Suppresses Wrath, answer us.
Answer us, You Who Dons Righteousness, answer us.
Answer us, King Who Reigns Over Kings, answer us.
Answer us, Awesome and Powerful One, answer us.
Answer us, You Who Forgives and Pardons, answer us.
Answer us, You Who Answers in Times of Distress, answer us.
Answer us, Redeemer and Rescuer, answer us.
Answer us, Righteous and Upright One, answer us.
Answer us, He Who is Close to Those Who Call Upon Him, answer us.
Answer us, Merciful and Gracious One, answer us.
Answer us, You Who Hears the Destitute, answer us.
Answer us, You Who Supports the Wholesome, answer us.
Answer us, You Who are Hard to Anger, answer us.
Answer us, You Who are Easy to Pacify, answer us.
Answer us, You Who Answers In a Time of Favor, answer us.
Answer us, Father of Orphans, answer us.
Answer us, Judge of Widows, answer us.

The Merciful One Who Answers the poor, may He answer us.
The Merciful One Who Answers the brokenhearted, may He answer us.
The Merciful One Who Answers the humble of spirit, may He answer us.

O Merciful One, answer us!
O Merciful One, have pity!
O Merciful One, have mercy upon us – now, swiftly, and soon!

Concluding Supplication

The following is recited seated.

And David said to Gad: "I am exceedingly distressed. Let us fall into The Lord's hand for His mercies are abundant, but let me not fall into human hands.

O compassionate and Gracious One, I have sinned before you, O Lord, Who is full of mercy, have mercy on me and accept my supplications.

Lord, do not rebuke me in Your anger nor chastise me in Your rage. Favor me, O Lord, for I am feeble. Heal me, O Lord, for my bones shudder. My soul is utterly confounded. And You, Lord, how long? Desist, Lord, release my soul – save me as befits your kindness, for there is no mention of you in death. In the lower world, who will thank you? I am wearied with my sigh, each night my tears drench my bed and soak my couch. My eye is dimmed by anger, aged by my tormentors. Depart from me all evildoers, for the Lord has heard the sound of my weeping! The Lord has heard my plea. The Lord will accept my prayer. Let all my foes be shamed and utterly confounded; they will regret and be ashamed.

The following is recited while standing:

We know not what we do, but our eyes are upon you. Remember your mercies, Lord, and your kindnesses, for they extend from the beginning of the world. May your kindness be upon us, O Lord, as we have awaited You. May your mercies meet us quickly. Be gracious to us O Lord! Amid rage, remember to be merciful! For He knows our nature; He remembers that we are dust. **All continue to the end; the Leader reads this last verse aloud:** Help us, O God of our salvation, for the sake of Your glory. Rescue us and judge us favorably!

Sanctification

Leader: May His great name be ever exalted and sanctified (**Cong.:** Amen!) **Leader:** in the world that He created according to His will. May His kingship reign in our lifetimes and in our days, swiftly and soon, and we say: Amen!

Cong.: Amen! May His great Name be blessed forever and ever!

Leader: May His great name be blessed forever and ever. Blessed, praised, glorified, exalted, extolled, mighty, upraised, and lauded is the name of the Holy One, Blessed is He (**Cong.:** Blessed is He!) exceedingly beyond any blessing and song or praise and consolation that may be uttered in the world, and we say: Amen (**Cong.:**. Amen!)

Selichos

The Second, Third, and Fourth Days

The service for these days differs slightly from that of the first day.

Opening Prayers

Sanctification

Leader: May His great name be ever exalted and sanctified (**Cong.:** Amen!) in the world that He created according to His will. May His kingship reign in our lifetimes and in our days, swiftly and soon, and we say: Amen!

Cong.: Amen! May His great Name be blessed forever and ever!

Leader: May His great name be blessed forever and ever. Blessed, praised, glorified, exalted, extolled, mighty, upraised, and lauded is the name of the Holy One, Blessed is He (**Cong.:** Blessed is He!) exceedingly beyond any blessing and song or praise and consolation that may be uttered in the world, and we say: Amen (**Cong.:**. Amen!)

All continue individually:

To you, Lord, is the righteousness...

To you, Lord, is the righteousness and to us the shamefacedness. What can we plead? What can we say? What can be uttered? How can we justify ourselves? We will search our ways, inspect them, and then we shall return to you, for Your right hand is outstretched to accept those who return. Neither with kindnesses nor worthy deeds do we come before You. Rather, like the poor and needy do we knock upon Your doors. We knock upon your doors, O Merciful and Compassionate One! Please, do not turn us away from You unanswered! Our King, do not turn us away from You unanswered, for You alone hear prayer!

All flesh shall come to You...

All flesh shall come to You, the One who hears prayer. All flesh shall come to bow before You, Lord. They will come and bow before you, my Lord, and will render honor unto Your name. Come! Let us prostrate ourselves and bow! Let us kneel before God, our maker. Let us come to His dwelling places, let us prostrate at His footstool. Enter His gates with thanksgiving and His courts with praise. Give thanks to Him and praise His name! Exalt the Lord, our God, and bow at His footstool for He is Holy. Exalt the Lord, our God, and bow at His holy mountain for holy is the Lord, our God. Prostrate yourselves before the Lord in His most holy place. Tremble before Him, all who are upon earth.

As for us, through Your abundant kindness we shall enter Your house. We shall prostrate ourselves toward Your holy sanctuary in awe of You.
We will bow towards Your holy sanctuary and give thanks to Your name, for Your kindness and truth, because You have exalted Your promise beyond Your name. Come! Let us sing to the Lord, let us call out unto the Rock of our salvation! Let

us greet Him with thanksgiving, let us call out to Him with praiseful songs. Let us share together in sweet counsel, let us walk in throngs within the house of God.

God is dreaded in the hidden-most counsel of the holy ones, inspiring awe upon all those who surround him. Lift your hands in the sanctuary and bless the Lord. Behold! Bless the Lord, all you servants of the Lord, who stand in the house of the Lord in the nights. For what force is there in heaven or earth comparable to Your deeds and power? For His is the sea and He perfected the dry land; His hands fashioned it. For in His power are the hidden mysteries of the earth; the mountain summits belong to Him. For the soul of every living thing is His — so too is the spirit of all human flesh. Heaven will gratefully praise Your wonders, O Lord. Your faithfulness [will be praised] in the assembly of holy ones. Your arm is great with power. You strengthen Your hand; You exalt Your right hand! The heavens are Yours and the earth too, the earth and its fullness, is yours for you founded them. You shattered the sea with your might; you smashed the heads of sea serpents upon the waters. You established order upon the earth; summer and winter — you fashioned them. You crushed the heads of the leviathan and You served it as food to the nation of legions. You split open fountain and stream, You dried the mighty rivers. The day is Yours and the night, as well, is Yours. You established luminaries and the sun — You, who performs great deeds that are beyond comprehension and wonders without number. For the Lord is a great God, a great king who is above all heavenly powers. For You are great and work wonders — You alone, O God. For Your kindness is exalted above the very heavens and Your truth is until the upper heavens. The Lord is great and exceedingly lauded. He is awesome above all heavenly powers. Yours, O Lord, is the greatness, strength, splendor, triumph, and glory — even everything in heaven and earth! Yours, O Lord is the dominion and sovereignty over every leader. Who could not revere You, O King of the Nations, for in all their kingdom there is none like You. There is none like You, O Lord, for You are great and Your name is great with power. The Lord, God of legions, who is like you, O Strong One, O God? Your faithfulness surrounds you! The Lord, Master of Legions, enthroned above the Cherubim, You alone are God.

Who can express the mighty acts of the Lord, who can announce all His praises? For what in the sky is comparable to the Lord, that can be likened to Him among the angels? What can we say before You who dwells on high? What can we say to You who abides in the highest heaven? What can we say before You, Lord, our God? What can we declare? What justification can we offer? We have no mouth with which to respond. Neither are we so brazen as to raise our heads, for our iniquities are too numerous to count and our sins too vast to be numbered. For Your Name's sake, O Lord, revive us and, with your righteousness, remove our souls from distress.

It is Your way, our God, to delay Your anger against people, both evil and good, and for this You are praised. Act for Your sake, our God, and not for ours.

Behold our condition – destitute and empty-handed. The soul is Yours and the body is Your handiwork; take pity on Your labor. **(All continue to the end, but The Leader concludes by reading the following sentences aloud:)** The soul is Yours and the body is Yours. O Lord, act for Your name's sake! We have come, relying upon Your name, Lord. Act for Your name's sake and because of Your name's glory – for "gracious and merciful God" is Your name! For your name's sake, O Lord, may You forgive our iniquity, abundant as it may be.

Cong. first aloud, then repeated aloud by Leader: Forgive us, our father, for in our abundant folly we have erred. Pardon us our king, for our iniquities are many.

All continue individually:

O God - You are slow to anger...

O God - You are slow to anger. You are called the Master of Mercy and You have taught the way of repentance. May You recall this day and every day the greatness of Your mercy and kindness. Turn to us in mercy for You are the Master of mercy. With supplication and prayer we approach Your presence. Turn back from Your anger. May we find shelter in the shadow of Your wings. Overlook sin and erase guilt. Give ear to our cry and be attentive to what we have said!

As a father...

As a father is merciful to his children, so too, Lord, may you have mercy upon us. The Lord, master of legions, praiseworthy is the person who trusts in You. Save, O Lord! May the King answer us on the day we call!

Leader: Forgive, please, our iniquity according to the greatness of your kindness! Forgive us as you granted forgiveness in your Holy Torah, as it is written:

Cong.: And said the Lord, "I have forgiven according to your word!"

Selicha – Psalms

On the second day, recite Psalm 62. On the third day, Psalm 75. On the fourth day, Psalm 51.

Standing, all recite:

Oh God, King, Who sites upon the throne of mercy...

Oh God, King, Who sits upon the throne of mercy, who acts with kindness, forgives iniquities, removes sin, and grants abundant pardon to careless transgressors and forgiveness to rebels – He Who deals righteously with every living being. You do not repay them according to their evil.

Leader: Please do not regard as sinful that which we have done foolishly and transgressed.

Cong.: We have erred, our Rock! Forgive us, O One who has formed us!
The following four verses are recited responsively. Each verse is recited first by the Leader followed by the Congregation:

Hear our voice... Hear our voice, O Lord, our God, show us pity and compassion, and accept our prayer with compassion and favor.

Bring us back to You O Lord, and we will return to you.

Do not cast us away from You, and do not remove Your holy spirit from us.

Do not cast us away in old age; do not forsake us when our strength is exhausted.

All continue individually:

Do not forsake us, Lord, our God, be not distant from us. Display for us a sign for good, so that our enemies may see it and be ashamed, for You, O Lord, will have helped and consoled us. To our sayings give ear, O Lord, perceive our thoughts. May the expressions of our mouth and the thoughts of our heart find favor before You, Lord, our Rock and our Redeemer. Because for You, Lord, we have waited; You will answer, my Lord, our God.

Confession

All continue individually:
Our God, may our prayer come before You. Do not ignore our supplication, for we are not so brazen and obstinate as to say before You, O Lord, our God, that we are righteous and have not sinned, for in truth we have sinned.

The confession is recited with head and body slightly bowed. Strike the left side of the chest with the right first at each bolded word.

WE have **become guilty**, we have **betrayed**, we have **robbed**, we have **spoken slander**, we have **caused perversion**, we have **caused wickedness**, we have **sinned willfully**, we have **extorted,** we have **accused falsely**, we have **given evil counsel**, we have **been deceitful**, we have **scorned**, we have **rebelled**, we have **provoked**, we have **turned away**, we have **been perverse**, we have **acted wantonly**, we have **persecuted**, we have **been obstinate**, we have **been wicked**, we have **corrupted**, we have **been abominable**, we have **strayed**, and You have let us go astray.

We have turned away from Your commandments and from Your good laws but to no avail. Yet, You are righteous in all that has come upon us, for You have acted truthfully while we have caused wickedness.

We have acted wickedly and sinned willfully. Inspire our hearts to abandon the path of evil, as it is written by Your prophet: May the wicked one abandon his way and the vicious man his thoughts; may he return to the Lord and He will show him mercy - to our God, for He is abundantly forgiving.

Your righteous anointed one [David] said before You: "Who can discern mistakes? From unperceived faults cleanse me." Cleanse us Lord, our God, of all our willful sins and purify us, of all our contaminations. Sprinkle upon us pure water and purify us, as it is written by Your prophet: I shall sprinkle pure water upon you and purify you; I will purify you of all your contaminations and of all your abominations.

Micah, your servant, said before You: "Who O God is like You, who pardons iniquity and overlooks transgression for the remnant of his heritage? He who has not retained His wrath eternally, for he desires kindness! He will again be merciful to us; He will suppress our iniquities and cast all sins into the depths of the sea."

Daniel, the greatly beloved man, cried out before You: "Incline Your ear, my God, and listen; open Your eyes and see our desolation and that of the city upon which Your Name is proclaimed. Not because of our righteousness do we cast our supplications before you, but rather because of your abundant compassion. O my Lord, heed! O my Lord, forgive! O my Lord, be attentive and act! Do not delay, for your sake my God, for your Name is proclaimed upon Your city and Your people."

Ezra the scribe said before You: My God, I am embarrassed and ashamed to lift my face to You, for our iniquities have multiplied and our sins have extended unto heaven. You are the God of forgiveness, compassionate and merciful, slow to anger, and abundant in kindness. You have not forsaken us.

Do not forsake us, our Father, do not cast us off, our Creator, do not abandon us, our Molder, and do not bring about our destruction.

Act for the sake... Act for the sake of Your truth, act for the sake of Your covenant, act for the sake of Your greatness and splendor, act for the sake of Your law, act for the sake of Your glory, act for the sake of Your meeting house, act for the sake of Your remembrance, act for the sake of Your kindness, act for the sake of Your goodness, act for the sake of Your oneness, act for the sake of Your honor, act for the sake of Your teaching, act for the sake of Your kingship, act for the sake of Your eternality, act for the sake of Your counsel, act for the sake of Your power, act for the sake of Your beauty, act for the sake of Your righteousness, act for the sake of Your sanctity, act for the sake of Your abundant mercy, act for the sake of Your presence, act for the sake of Your praise, act for the sake of Your beloved ones who rest in the dust, act for the sake of the desolation of your temple, act for the sake of the ruins of your altar, act for the sake of the martyrs for your holy name; act for the sake of those slaughtered for your oneness, act for the sake of those who entered fire and water for the sanctification of your name, act for the nursing infants who did not err act for the sake of the weaned babes who did not sin, act for the sake of the children at the schoolroom. Act for your sake, if not for ours. Act for your sake and save us!

Answer us...

Answer us, O Lord, answer us.
Answer us, Our God, answer us.
Answer us, Our Father, answer us.
Answer us, Our Creator, answer us.
Answer us, Our Redeemer, answer us.
Answer us, He Who Searches Us Out, answer us.
Answer us, Faithful God, answer us.
Answer us, Steadfast and Kind One, answer us.
Answer us, Pure and Upright One, answer us.
Answer us, Living and Enduring One, answer us.
Answer us, Good and Beneficent One, answer us.
Answer us, You Who Knows Inclination, answer us.
Answer us, You Who Suppresses Wrath, answer us.
Answer us, You Who Dons Righteousness, answer us.
Answer us, King Who Reigns Over Kings, answer us.
Answer us, Awesome and Powerful One, answer us.
Answer us, You Who Forgives and Pardons, answer us.
Answer us, You Who Answers in Times of Distress, answer us.
Answer us, Redeemer and Rescuer, answer us.
Answer us, Righteous and Upright One, answer us.
Answer us, He Who is Close to Those Who Call Upon Him, answer us.
Answer us, Merciful and Gracious One, answer us.
Answer us, You Who Hears the Destitute, answer us.
Answer us, You Who Supports the Wholesome, answer us.
Answer us, You Who are Hard to Anger, answer us.
Answer us, You Who are Easy to Pacify, answer us.
Answer us, You Who Answers In a Time of Favor, answer us.
Answer us, Father of Orphans, answer us.
Answer us, Judge of Widows, answer us.

The Merciful One Who Answers the poor, may He answer us.
The Merciful One Who Answers the brokenhearted, may He answer us.
The Merciful One Who Answers the humble of spirit, may He answer us.

O Merciful One, answer us!
O Merciful One, have pity!
O Merciful One, have mercy upon us – now, swiftly, and soon!

Concluding Supplication

The following is recited seated.

And David said to Gad: "I am exceedingly distressed. Let us fall into the Lord's hand for His mercies are abundant, but let me not fall into human hands.

O compassionate and Gracious One, I have sinned before you, Lord Who is full of mercy, have mercy on me and accept my supplications.

Lord, do not rebuke me in Your anger nor chastise me in Your rage. Favor me, O Lord, for I am feeble. Heal me, Lord, for my bones shudder. My soul is utterly confounded. And You, O Lord, how long? Desist Lord, release my soul – save me as befits Your kindness, for there is no mention of You in death. In the lower world, who will thank You? I am wearied with my sigh, each night my tears drench my bed and soak my couch. My eye is dimmed by anger, aged by my tormentors. Depart from me all evildoers, for the Lord has heard the sound of my weeping! The Lord has heard my plea. The Lord will accept my prayer. Let all my foes be shamed and utterly confounded; they will regret and be ashamed.

The following is recited while standing:

We know not what we do, but our eyes are upon you. Remember your mercies, O Lord, and your kindnesses, for they extend from the beginning of the world. May your kindness be upon us, O Lord, as we have awaited You. May your mercies meet us quickly. Be gracious to us, Lord! Amid rage, remember to be merciful! For He knows our nature; He remembers that we are dust. **All continue to the end; the Leader reads this last verse aloud:** Help us, O God of our salvation, for the sake of Your glory. Rescue us and judge us favorably!

Sanctification

Leader: May His great name be ever exalted and sanctified (**Cong.:** Amen!) **Leader:** in the world that He created according to His will. May His kingship reign in our lifetimes and in our days, swiftly and soon, and we say: Amen!

Cong.: Amen! May His great Name be blessed forever and ever!

Leader: May His great name be blessed forever and ever. Blessed, praised, glorified, exalted, extolled, mighty, upraised, and lauded is the name of the Holy One, Blessed is He (**Cong.:** Blessed is He!) exceedingly beyond any blessing and song or praise and consolation that may be uttered in the world, and we say: Amen (**Cong.:.** Amen!)

Pirchei Publishing
164 Village Path / P.O. Box 708
Lakewood, New Jersey 08701
(732) 370-3344
www.shulchanaruch.com

Product Produced & Compiled by YPS:
Rabbi Shaul Danyiel & Rabbi Ari Montanari
www.lionsden.info/YPS

THE YESHIVA PIRCHEI SHOSHANIM SHULCHAN ARUCH LEARNING PROJECT

The Noahide Laws – Lesson Twenty Eight

164 Village Path, Lakewood NJ 08701 732.370.3344
164 Rabbi Akiva, Bnei Brak, 03.616.6340

Outline of This Lesson:

1. Introduction

2. Judgment & Celebration

3. *Mitzvos* vs. *Minhagim*

4. Eve of Rosh HaShanah

5. Suggested Evening Prayers

6. Rosh HaShanah Night Meal

Festivals III: Rosh HaShanah

Lesson
28

Introduction

Rosh HaShanah, the Day of Judgment, Birthday of the World – it is a time of tremendous celebration and tremendous solemnity. It is a day of ultimate connection with the Creator.

Judgment & Celebration.

As we mentioned earlier, Rosh HaShanah is both a day of solemnity and rejoicing. We celebrate the completion of creation and the birthday of all mankind. However, it is also a day of judgment and solemnity for it is the day upon which Adam and Eve failed in their mission.

The observances of Rosh HaShanah strive to acknowledge the day's dual nature.

Shofar on Rosh HaShanah?

The general rule with all Noahide practice is to avoid imitating those commandments ordered only to the Jewish people. Besides the fact that such imitation-of-practice limits the universal aspect of Noahism, it also creates serious problems in Torah law. Therefore, Noahides should not blow the shofar on Rosh HaShanah.

Mitzvos vs. Minhagim

Mitzvos are those matters that God commanded to mankind, whether Noahide or Jew. However, *mihangim* (usually translated as "customs") are practices developed by man to enhance the spiritual experience of the holidays. While the law is that Noahides may not take on Jewish mitzvos (unless they provide some practical, real-world benefit; i.e. *Tzedaka* or honoring one's parents), Noahides may certainly take on established Jewish *minhagim*.

These *minhagim* are often rich with meaning and speak deeply to the human experience of the Torah. We will mention many such *minhagim* in the course of these lessons.

Eve of Rosh HaShanah

Rosh HaShanah, as all of the Torah's festivals, beings at sunset on the previous evening. For example, Rosh HaShana 2015 is on Monday, September 14. However, it actually beings at sunset on Sunday, September 13.

By Rosh HaShanah eve, the house should be cleaned in honor of the holiday. One should also endeavor to get a haircut, cut his nails, and dress in clean, nice clothing to welcome the Great Day.

One should not rush into Rosh HaShanah. Instead, all of the preparations should be completed well before sunset so that one may enter the day in a spirit of peace, tranquility, and focus.

Evening Prayers

As with all of the liturgies brought in this course, they are based on the traditional Jewish prayers, yet adapted as needed for Noahide use. These prayer services are by no means the final or definitive forms of these prayers. Instead, these services are intended as a starting point for growth and development.

Introductory Psalm

Psalm 96
The Leader reads the bold text aloud.

Sing to The Lord a new song! Sing to The Lord, all the Earth! Praise The Lord and bless His name! Announce His salvation from day to day! Declare His honor among the nations and His wonders among all peoples. For the Lord is great and exceedingly praised; He is feared above all gods. For all the gods of the nations are worthless – but The Lord made the heavens! Majesty and glory are before him, strength and beauty are in His sanctuary. Render to The Lord, you families of the nations, render to The Lord glory and honor! Give The Lord the honor due to his Name. Bring offerings into His courtyards. Bow down before the Lord in abundant holiness and tremble before Him, everyone on Earth! Say among the nations, "The Lord reigns!" The world is firmly set, it shall not falter. He will judge the nations in righteousness.

Heaven will rejoice and the Earth will be glad! The oceans and their fullness will roar! The fields and all that is in them will exult! **The trees of the forest will sing with joy before the Lord – For He will have arrived, He will have come to judge the Earth. He judges the world in righteousness and the peoples in His truth!**

Introductory Nighttime Psalm & Verses of Praise[1]

A Song of Ascents: Behold, bless The Lord, all you servants of the Lord who stand in the House of the Lord in the nights. Lift your hands in the Sanctuary and bless the Lord. May the Lord bless you from Zion, the Maker of heaven and earth.[2]

In perfect peace I will lie down and sleep; for You, O Lord, will set me apart and secure my dwelling.[3] At dawn, the Lord will command His kindness; at night His resting place is with me – a prayer to the God of my life![4] The salvation of the righteous is from the Lord; their might in a time

---

[1] Inclusion of these Psalm verses is adapted from *Nusach Sfard*, the Chassidic rite version of the *siddur*.

[2] Psalm 134.

[3] Ibid. 4:9.

[4] Ibid. 42:9.

of distress. The Lord helps them and enables their escape; He enables their escape from the wicked and will save them, for they have taken refuge in Him.[5]

Sanctification

Leader: May His great name be ever exalted and sanctified (**Cong.:** Amen!) in the world that He created according to His will. May His kingship reign in our lifetimes and in our days, swiftly and soon, and we say: Amen!

Cong.: Amen! May His great Name be blessed forever and ever!

Leader: May His great name be blessed forever and ever. Blessed, praised, glorified, exalted, extolled, mighty, upraised, and lauded is the name of the Holy One, Blessed is He (**Cong.:** Blessed is He!) exceedingly beyond any blessing and song or praise and consolation that may be uttered in the world, and we say: Amen (**Cong.:.** Amen!)

Call to Prayer (omitted by one praying alone)

Leader: Blessed is The Lord, the Blessed One!
Cong.: Blessed is The Lord, the Blessed One, for all eternity!
Leader: Blessed is The Lord, the Blessed One, for all eternity!

Acceptance of Kingship

All aloud: Almighty God, we accept upon ourselves Your sovereign kingship and mastery:

All continue individually:

> You alone are our God,
> You alone are our King,
> You alone are omnipotent, and
> You alone are eternal.
>
> You alone are our creator,
> You alone are our savior.
> You alone do we worship, and to

---

[5] Ibid. 37:39 – 40.

You alone do we give thanks.

As it is written in Your holy Torah: "You shall know this day and take unto your heart that God alone is God; in the heavens above and upon the earth below – there is none other!"[6] And, "You shall love your God with all your heart, all your soul, and all your means,"[7] and to (**Leader recites aloud:**) **"Fear God, your God, and serve Him, and to vow in His name only."**[8]

Leader: The Lord shall reign for all eternity![9]
Cong: The Lord shall reign for all eternity!

Silent Prayer

During the silent Prayer, all should stand erect with the feet together. One should pray only loud enough to hear himself.

On God's Might

Your might is eternal, my Lord, the one who resuscitates the dead, who is abundant in salvations, who sustains the living with kindness, who revives the dead with abundant mercy, who supports the fallen, heals the sick, and releases the bound, Who upholds his faith to those who sleep in the dust. Who is like you, O Master of mighty deeds?

Who is comparable to You, O King, who causes death and restores life, who makes salvation bloom?

And You are faithful to revive the dead! Blessed are you, O Lord, who revives the dead!

On God's Holiness

You are holy and Your Name is Holy, and the holy ones praise you every day, eternally. Therefore, bestow your awe upon all Your works and your dread upon all you have created. Let all your works revere you and all creations prostrate themselves before you. Let them all whole-heartedly

---

[6] Deut. 4:39.

[7] Deut. 6:5.

[8] Deut. 6:13.

[9] Exodus 15:18.

do your will. For, as we know HaShem our God, the dominion is yours. Might is in your hand and strength within your right hand; your name invokes awe upon all that you have created.

You are Holy and your name is awesome, and there is no god other than You, as it is written: The Lord, Master of Legions, will be exalted in judgment, and the Holy God will be sanctified in righteousness. Blessed are you, O Lord, the Holy king.

On the Day of Judgment

Our God, may there arise, come, reach, be noted, be favored, be heard, be considered, and be remembered a remembrance of ourselves before you for deliverance, for goodness, for grace, for kindness and compassion, for life, and for peace upon this Day of Judgment. Remember us on it, O Lord, for blessing and for life.
Be gracious and compassionate with us, favor us for salvation, compassion, and pity, for our eyes are turned to you, for you are God, the gracious and compassionate King!

Our God, reign over the entire universe in Your glory. Be exalted over the entire world in Your splendor. Reveal Yourself, in the majestic grandeur of Your strength, upon all that dwell within Your world. Let everything that has been made know that You are its maker and let everything that has been shaped understand that you are its sculptor. Let everything with the breath of life in its nostrils proclaim: "The Lord is King! His Kingship rules above all!" O God, purify our hearts to serve You sincerely, for You are the true God and Your word is true and eternal! Look down upon Your creation and judge it favorably! Grant us the opportunity to return to you! Grant us life, grant us salvation, and grant us favor! Blessed are you, O Lord, King over all, who sanctifies the Day of Judgment!

Giving Thanks

We thank you, for it is you who are The Lord, our God, and the Rock of our Lives. We shall thank You and relate Your praise for our lives, which are committed to Your power, and for our souls that are entrusted to You, for Your miracles that are with us every day, and for Your wonders and favors in every time – Morning, noon, and night. The Benevolent One, for Your benevolences were never exhausted, and The Compassionate One, for Your compassions are never ending – we place our hope in You.

Please, inscribe us all for a good life!

And all life will thank You and praise Your name, O God of salvation and help. Blessed are you, O Lord, Your Name is "The Benevolent one" and to You alone is it fitting to offer thanks!

For Peace

Establish peace upon the world and upon all peoples, for you are king, the master of peace!

May we be remembered and inscribed before You in the book of life, blessing, peace, and livelihood.

Blessed are you, O Lord, who creates peace.

Concluding Supplication

My God, guard my tongue from evil and my lips from speaking deceit. To those who would curse me, let my soul be silent; let my soul be like dust to all. Open my heart to your will so that my soul will pursue it. As for all those plan evil against me, quickly nullify their counsel, frustrate their designs. Act for Your Name's sake, act for Your right-hand's sake, act for Your sanctity's sake. Let Your right hand save and respond to me.

May the expressions of my mouth and the thoughts of my heart find favor before you, Lord, my Rock and my Redeemer.

One takes three steps back at this point, as if taking leave of a king.

Bow to the left and say: He who makes peace in His heights,
Bow to the right and say: May He Make peace upon us,
Bow forward and say: And upon the entire world.
One straightens and concludes: And we say: Amen.

Remain in place for a moment, and then take three steps forward. The silent prayer is concluded.

Psalm 24

When the majority of those present have concluded their silent prayer, the leader begins the following responsive recitation. The Psalm is recited responsively, verse by verse, Leader followed by Congregation

Of David: a Psalm. The Lord's is the earth and its fullness, the inhabited land, and all those who dwell upon it.

For He founded it upon the seas, established it upon the rivers.

Who may ascend the Lord's mountain, and who may stand in the place of His Holiness?

One of clean hands and of pure heart, who has neither sworn in vain by My soul, nor deceitfully.

He will receive a blessing from The Lord and righteousness from the God of his salvation.

This is the generation of those who seek Him, those who strive for Your Presence.

Raise up your heads, O Gates! Be uplifted, O eternal entrances, so that the King of glory may enter!

Who is this king of glory? The Lord – the powerful and mighty! The Lord – Who is great in battle!

Raise up your heads, O Gates! Be uplifted, O eternal entrances, so that the King of glory may enter!

Who is this king of Glory? The Lord, the Master of Legions, He is the king of glory! Selah!

We Bend Our Knees...

One should bend the knees and bow down at the words in bold text, straitening up at ...King of kings...

We **bend our knee, bow down**, and give thanks, before the King of kings, the Holy One blessed is He, Who stretches forth the heavens and founded the earth, Whose honored abode is in the heavens above, and Whose powerful presence is in the most exalted heights. He is our God; there is none else. True is our king, and there is nothing besides Him, as it is written in His Torah: "Know this day and take to your heart that the Lord is God; in the heaven above and on the earth below - there is none other."

Therefore, we place our hope in You, Lord our God, that we may soon behold your mighty splendor; to banish idolatry from the earth. False gods will be utterly cut off; to perfect the world through the Almighty's sovereignty. All humanity shall call in Your Name, returning the wicked of the world unto you. Then all the inhabitants of the world will recognize and know that to you every knee should bend and to Your Name every tongue should pledge. Before You, Lord our God, they will bow and prostrate themselves, and render honor unto the glory of Your Name; they will all accept upon themselves the yoke of Your kingship so that You may reign over them, soon, forever and ever. For the kingdom is Yours and You will reign in all eternity, as it is written in Your Torah: "The Lord will reign forever and ever." And it is said: **"The Lord will be King over all the world – on that day the Lord will be One and His Name will be One."**

Psalm 27

Each congregant recites psalm 27 to his or herself. The leader recites the opening and concluding verses (in bold text) aloud.

Of David: The Lord is my light[10] **and my salvation.**[11] **Of whom shall I be afraid?** The Lord is the strength of my life. Of whom shall I dread? When evil-doers – my tormentors and opponents[12] – draw near to devour my flesh, it is they who stumble and fall. Though an army may besiege me, my heart will not fear. Should warfare arise against me, in this alone I shall trust.[13]

I have asked one thing of The Lord, only this have I sought: that I may dwell in the house of The Lord all the days of my life, to behold the pleasantness of The Lord, and to meditate within His sanctuary.[14]

On the day of evil He will hide me within His shelter. He will conceal me in the innermost shelter of his tent. He will lift me up upon a rock. And now he will raise

---

[10] The Midrash understands this as a reference to Rosh HaShanah.

[11] The salvation mentioned here is the atonement of the holiday season. For Jews it refers to the atonement of Yom Kippur, for Noahides the atonement of Sukkot.

[12] The evil-doers and opponents mentioned in this psalm are primarily internal. They are the devices of the *yetzer ha-ra*, the evil inclination. They are also the memories and emotions associated with one's past misdeeds. These memories often torment a person and hamper their ability to return to G-d. This will be discussed more in a future lesson.

[13] Rashi and Radak explain that this refers to the opening line "HaShem is my light and my salvation," which is the process of Rosh HaShanah and subsequent atonement. One must trust in this process. Once a person has returned to HaShem and reestablished a positive relationship with G-d, G-d will protect and shelter him. Alternatively, Ibn Ezra explains that this phrase refers to the next sentence: *I have asked one thing of HaShem, only this have I sought: that I may dwell in the house of HaShem all the days of my life...* One should trust in G-d because he (the penitent) ultimately desires spiritual success and not the vain achievements of this world.

[14] Writes the Malbim, that despite the many desires and needs a person may have, the desire to know his creator is the ultimate, all inclusive desire of the soul.

my head above my foes that surround me. I will slaughter in His tent joyous offerings. I will sing and make music to The Lord. O Lord, hear my voice when I call! Favor me and answer me! For your sake has my heart spoke to me: "Seek his presence!" O God, I seek your presence! Do not conceal your countenance from me! Do not repel your servant in anger! You have been my help. Do not forsake me, do not abandon me, O God of my salvation!

Though my father and mother have abandoned me,[15] The Lord shall gather me in. Teach me your way, O Lord, and on account of my watchful foes[16] set me upon a straight path. Do not give me over to their wishes for they have set against me false witnesses who breathe violence.

Had I not believed[17] that I would see the goodness of the Lord in the land of life![18] Hope to the Lord! Be strong and He will give you courage[19] – and hope to the Lord!

Greetings

The traditional greeting for Rosh HaShanah is:

May you be inscribed and sealed, immediately, for a good life and for peace.

And,

A good and sweet year!

---

[15] Sforno explains that once a person becomes an adult he must find his own way in the world. He can no longer rely upon his parents to make choices for him. He must choose his values and make his own decisions. Although his parents are no longer his guiding voice, HaShem is always there. HaShem is eternally our father and guide.

[16] The Hebrew here is a little difficult to translate. The word for "Watchful foes" is related to the word for "staring" or "gazing." In the context of our verse, it refers to those who stare maliciously. The psalm is asking G-d to frustrate the wishes of those who maliciously watch and mock one who wishes to come back to G-d. See Radak.

[17] Rashi explains: Were it not for my faith in G-d, my enemies would have destroyed me and I would have never merited to achieve closeness to G-d.

[18] Meaning the World to Come. See *Brachos* 4a.

[19] Strength in faith is the ultimate source of all courage.

Night Meal

The Blessing on bread is made by the leader on 1 loaf on behalf of all present.
The custom is to use a round loaf during the holiday season.

Leader: Blessed are You, O Lord, our God, King of the Universe, who brings forth bread from the Earth **(Guests: Amen!)**

While still holding the loaf, the leader recites:

Leader: Blessed are you, HaShem, our God, who has kept us alive, sustained us, and brought us to this season! **(Guests: Amen!)**

The loaf is then cut and distributed. Each person should eat his or her slice with honey. One should refrain from speaking from after answering "Amen" until having partaken of the bread.

Simanim - Signs

The custom of Simanim *involves eating foods whose names or qualities invoke positive thoughts and ideas of blessing. On Rosh HaShanah, God looks into the heart of all peoples and renders judgment. Therefore, one's mind and heart should only look for the positive on Rosh HaShanah. To set the tone for the Rosh HaShanah meal, the custom of* Simanim *is placed at its beginning.*

The source of the custom is found in the Talmud:

> *Abaye taught: Since you have said that a* Siman *(the name or quality of an item) holds significance, a person should habituate himself at the start of each year to eat gourds, fenugreek, leeks, beets, and dates.*[20]

The foods listed here are important because their names or other qualities invoke concepts of blessings.

Therefore, Jews have the custom to eat foods for Simanim *whose names invoke positive qualities, or that taste sweet, or that have traits that are considered blessed.*

There is no fixed order or list of Simanim *foods; indeed, many families even invent their own!*

Below is an example of a traditional Simanim *order. Only the first* Siman*, apples, is universal.*

---

[20] *Horayos* 12a; *Kerisus* 6a.

Apples

Every guest takes a piece of apple, dips it in honey, and then each guest makes the following blessing for his or herself:

Blessed are You, The Lord, our God, King of the universe, who creates the fruit of the tree.

A small bit of the apple is eaten following this blessing. Then the leader then recites:

Leader: May it be your will, Lord our God, that you renew us for a good and sweet year! **(Guests: Amen)**

Carrot or Fenugreek[21]

Each participant then takes a small piece of carrot or fenugreek. The leader recites:

Leader: May it be your will, Lord, our God, that our merits increase! **(Guests: Amen)**

Beets[22]

Each participant takes a piece of beet and the leader recites:

Leader: May it be your will, HaShem our God, that our adversaries be removed from upon us. **(Guests: Amen)**

Pomegranate

Leader: May it be your will, HaShem our God, that our merits increase like the seeds of a pomegranate. **(Guests: Amen)**

Fish

Leader: May it be your will, HaShem our God, that we be fruitful and multiply like the fish of the sea. **(Guests: Amen)**

There are many, many, more Simanim *that are, like these, based on Aramaic, Hebrew, or Yiddish wordplay. It is appropriate for Noahides to add more based on their own languages. Some people, in fact, eat raisins, praying for a "raise in…," followed by celery, for "salary!"*

The only general rules for Simanim *are: no bitter or sharp tasting foods, and that the prayer formula:* May it be your will, Lord, our God… *is recited before each* Siman *is eaten.*

---

[21] The reason for this *Simon* is that the Yiddish word for carrots is *mehren*, which also means *to increase*. Fenugreek is *rubya* in Aramaic, which also implies abundance and increase.

[22] Beets, in Aramaic, is *silka*. This is similar to the world *salek*, which means *to remove from upon*.

Words of Torah

During the course of the meal, those present should be careful not to speak ill of anyone or anything, focusing only on good things and good thoughts. The discussion should include much Torah, goals for the New Year, and prayers and blessings for spiritual and material successes.

Blessing After the Meal

Psalm 67[23]

For the Conductor upon the *Neginos*, a Psalm, a song: May God favor us and bless us, may He illuminate His countenance with us, *Selah*. To make known Your way upon the earth, among all the nations Your salvation. Then peoples will acknowledge You, O God, the peoples will acknowledge You – all of them. Nations will be glad and sing for Joy, because you will judge the peoples fairly and guide with fairness the nations on the earth, Selah! Then peoples will acknowledge you, O God, the peoples will acknowledge You – all of them! The earth will then have yielded its produce, may God, our God, bless us, May God bless us, and may all the ends of the earth fear him!

At the conclusion of the meal, the following blessing is recited either by all together, each person to him or herself, or by the leader on behalf of all present, who respond "Amen."

Blessed is the God of the universe of Whose bounty we have eaten.

---

[23] The Jewish practice is to recite Psalm 126 before concluding the meal. This psalm expresses the hope for redemption of the Jewish people. Psalm 67, however, is more appropriate for Noahides because it refers to the entire world and its peoples coming to know God. It also refers to God as the source of all blessing, food, and produce.

THE YESHIVA PIRCHEI SHOSHANIM SHULCHAN ARUCH LEARNING
PROJECT

The Noahide Laws – Lesson Twenty Nine

164 Village Path, Lakewood NJ 08701 732.370.3344
164 Rabbi Akiva, Bnei Brak, 03.616.6340

Outline of This Lesson:

1. Introduction

2. Yom Kippur & History

3. The Offerings of Sukkot

4. Sources of Judgment

5. *Nisukh HaMayim* – The Water Libation

6. Summary So Far

7. Sukkot & Yom Kippur

8. Tying it All Together

Festivals III: Sukkot

Lesson

29

Introduction

The Festivals of the Torah and their meanings transcend any particular time or place. Nevertheless, each of the holidays is anchored to some event in history. Yom Kippur is the most important Jewish holiday after Rosh HaShanah. However, its historical anchor and meaning are both unique to Israel alone. The purpose and theme of Yom Kippur, though, has a universal parallel in the holiday of Sukkot. Furthermore, the historical anchor of Sukkot is directly related to Noahism.

Yom Kippur & History

On the 7th day of Sivan, Moses ascended Sinai and remained there for 40 days and 40 nights (See Rashi to Ex. 32:1). At the end of this period, Moses received the first set of tablets (Ex. 31:18).

On the 16th of Tammuz, the Jewish people construct the Golden Calf (Ex. 32:1 – 5; See Rashi). They began worshiping it on the following morning (Ex. 32:6). God commands Moses to descend on that day, the 17th of Tammuz. Upon seeing the people's transgression, Moses cast down the tablets, breaking them against the mountain. He grinds the calf into dust; mixing it with water and makes the people drink it. The Levites are commanded to kill all of the transgressors (Ex. 32:7 – 9).

On the 19th of Tammuz, Moses ascends the mountain again (Ex. 32:30 – 34). During this ascent, Moses secured a tentative pardon for the people.

He descended at the end of 40 days, on the 29th of Av, to inform the people of this.

On the 1st of Elul, Moses ascended the mountain for a third time Ex. (34:4-17). During this third 40-day ascent, Moses finally achieved pardon for the Jewish people (Ex. 33:17, 8-10). At the end of this period, Moses descended with the second set of tablets (Ex. 34:1-2, 27 – 29). The date of this descent was the 10ᵗʰ of Tishrei – Yom Kippur.

This day would be designated as a day of atonement for the Jewish people for all times:

> *This shall remain for you an eternal decree: In the seventh month, on the tenth day of the month, you shall afflict yourselves and you shall not do any work, neither the native nor the convert among you, for on this day He shall provide atonement for you to cleanse you from your sins – before the Lord you shall be cleansed.*[1]

Yom Kippur's general theme, atonement, is anchored in the history of the Jewish people and the sin of the golden calf.

Being anchored in the historical experience of Israel and, being commanded only to Israel, Yom Kippur only provides atonement for Israel. As such, it is not a Noahide holiday and, therefore, does not have any relevance to Noahides. Does this mean, then, that Noahides have no means of atonement? No – it does not. God designated another time for Noahide atonement.

The Offerings of Sukkot

As we have mentioned several times in previous lessons, many of the Torah's festivals have both universal meanings and specific meanings. The specific meanings of the festivals pertain only to the Jewish people. The universal meanings, however, are for the entire world. It is these latter, universal meanings which are the festival's meaning for Noahides.

The Mishnah tells us:

> *At four junctures, the world is judged: on Passover for grain, on Shavuot for fruits, on Rosh Hashanah all pass before him like sheep of the flock, as it is written, "He form their hearts as one, he understands all of their deeds." (Psalms 33).* **On Sukkot, the world is judged for water.**[2]

This Mishnah is teaching us the universally relevant themes of these holidays. For Sukkot, as we see, the theme is judgment for water. Superficially, this may seem

---

[1] Leviticus 16:29-30.

[2] *Mishnah, Rosh HaShanah* 1:2.

like an awfully narrow concept. However, there is much more going on than meets the eye. Let's start with the offerings given on the days of Sukkot:

[Day 1:] And on the fifteenth day of the seventh month, there shall be a holy convocation for you; you shall not perform any mundane work, and you shall celebrate a festival to the Lord for seven days. You shall offer up a burnt offering, a fire offering for a spirit of satisfaction to the Lord: **thirteen young bulls**, *two rams, fourteen lambs in the first year; they shall [all] be unblemished. And their meal offering [shall be] fine flour mixed with oil; three tenths for each bull for the thirteen bulls, two tenths for each ram for the two rams. And one tenth for each lamb, for the fourteen lambs. And one young male goat for a sin offering, besides the continual burnt offering, its meal offering, and its libation.*

[Day 2:] And on the second day, **twelve young bulls**, *two rams, and fourteen lambs in the first year, [all] unblemished. And their meal offerings and their libations, for the bulls, for the rams, and for the lambs, according to their number, as prescribed. And one young male goat for a sin offering, besides the continual burnt offering, its meal offering, and their libations.*

[Day 3:] And on the third day, **eleven bulls**, *two rams, and fourteen lambs in the first year, [all] unblemished. And their meal offerings and their libations, for the bulls, for the rams, and for the lambs, according to their number, as prescribed. And one young male goat for a sin offering, besides the continual burnt offering, its meal offering and its libation.*

[Day 4:] And on the fourth day, **ten bulls**, *two rams, and fourteen lambs in the first year, [all] unblemished. Their meal offerings and their libations, for the bulls, for the rams, and for the lambs, according to their number, as prescribed. And one young male goat for a sin offering, besides the continual burnt offering, its meal offering and its libation.*

[Day 5:] And on the fifth day **nine bulls**, *two rams, and fourteen lambs in the first year, [all] unblemished. And their meal offerings and their libations, for the bulls, for the rams, and for the lambs, according to their number, as prescribed. And one young male goat for a sin offering, besides the continual burnt offering, its meal offering, and its libation.*

[Day 6:] And on the sixth day, **eight bulls**, *two rams, and fourteen lambs in the first year, [all] unblemished. And their meal offerings and their libations, for the bulls, for the rams, and for the lambs, according to their number, as prescribed. And one young male goat for a sin offering, besides the continual burnt offering, its meal offering, and its libations.*

*[Day 7:] And on the seventh day, **seven bulls**, two rams and fourteen lambs in the first year, [all] unblemished. And their meal offerings and their libations, for the bulls, for the rams, and for the lambs, according to their number, as prescribed for them. One young male goat for a sin offering, besides the continual burnt offering, its meal offering, and its libation.[3]*

As you may have noticed, the number of offerings remains essentially the same each day with the exception of the bull offering. Each day of Sukkot, the bull offering is reduced by one. The total number of the offerings is 70: 13 + 12 + 11 + 10 + 9 + 8 + 7 = 70. Why 70?

Sukkot 55b

Rabbi Eliezer said: "To what do these 70 bulls correspond? They correspond to the 70 nations of the world." …

Rabbi Yochanan said: "Woe to the non-Jews who don't even realize what they lost! As long as the temple stood, the altar atoned for them…

Rabbi Eliezer is telling us that the 70 bulls were offered by Israel as atonement for the 70 nations of the world. Rabbi Yochanan laments that the non-Jews who destroyed the temple didn't realize what they were losing: it was the temple that gained them divine forgiveness and atonement each year through the bull offerings!

Sources of Judgment

Braisa, Talmud Rosh HaShana 16a

Rabbi Yehuda said in the name of Rabbi Akiva: Why did the Torah tell us to bring the Omer offering on Passover [see Lev. 23:9-14]? Because Passover is the time for judgment on grain. The Holy One, Blessed is He, said "Bring before me the Omer on Passover so that the produce in the fields will be blessed for you." Why did the Torah tell us to bring the two loaves on Shavuot [Lev. 23:17]?[4] Because Shavuot is the time

---

[3] Num. 29:12-34

[4] The offering brought on Shavuot was from wheat, which is not actually a fruit. However, the two wheat loaves were brought as a prerequisite to the bikkurim, the offering of first fruits. Alternatively, it could be that this Braisa is according to Rabbi Yehuda's own opinion that the tree from which Adam and Eve ate was a "wheat tree." According to many, bread grew directly from trees before the sin of Adam. It was only afterwards that wheat was diminished, requiring harvesting, winnowing, grinding, and baking. See Machshavos Charutz 60; Sanhedrin 70b and Eyn Yaakov there. Therefore, wheat is offered as atonement for man's original sin of eating from the tree. It is by this mechanic that the wheat offering of Shavuot provides good judgment upon the fruit trees.

for judgment on the fruits of the trees. The Holy One blessed is He, said: "Bring before me the two loaves on Shavuot so that the fruits of the tree will be blessed for you."

Why did the Torah tell us to pour water libations on Sukkot? Because the Holy One, Blessed is He, said: pour water before me on Sukkot so that the rains may be blessed for you...

This *braisa* is telling us that the offering commanded on each holiday hints to the judgment of that holiday. Now, for each of the festivals mentioned here, as well as for Rosh HaShanah, there are verses in the Torah that allude to the festival offering. The one exception is Sukkot. Our *braisa* tells us about a water libation on sukkot. What is this and why is it not mentioned in the Torah?

Nisukh HaMayim – The Water Libation

In the times of the temple, every peace offerings and burnt offering was accompanied by a flour offering and a wine libation. On Sukkot, however, there was an additional libation of water. This water libation, the *Nisukh ha-Mayim*, was poured upon the altar at the giving of the morning sacrifice. This offering consisted of two stages: the *Semichas beis ha-shoeivah* (water drawing ceremony), and the actual *Nisukh ha-Mayim* (pouring of the water).

Each morning, the Levites and Kohanim drew three *lugin* of fresh water with a golden vessel from the Shiloach, a stream that ran to the south of the Temple mount.

The ceremony of drawing water for the libation was an occasion for tremendous joy. The Talmud states:

One who has not witnessed the celebration of water-drawing has never seen real joy.[5]

The joy was so great that even brought some to the spirit of prophecy:

Why is the celebration called beis ha-sho'evah *[the celebration of the place of water drawing]? Because from there [from the ceremony itself] one draws the spirit of holiness. .. Yonah ben Amitai was one of the pilgrims who ascended to Jerusalem on the Festival. He went to the* Semichas bet ha-sho'evah *and [from the intense joy] the spirit of holiness rested upon him and he attained prophecy. This teaches us that the spirit of holiness rests upon a person only when his heart is filled with joy.*[6]

---

[5] *Sukkah* 51a.

[6] *Yerushalmi Sukkah* 5:1.

Following the water drawing was the libation ceremony itself, which was also celebrated with great fanfare.

However, the ceremony of the water libation is not mentioned anywhere in the Torah. The sages tell us that this *mitzvah* is a *Halacha le-Moshe mi-Sinai*, a direct commandment given to Moses at Sinai. It is part of the *Torah SheBaal Peh* – the Oral Torah.

Summary So Far

Let's look at what we know so far:

- On Sukkot a water offering was given – the *Nisukh ha-Mayim*.

- Following the lead of the *braisa* mentioned above, this would indicate that the world is judged for water on Sukkot.

- Unlike the offerings associated with all other festivals, this offering was given as part of the *Torah SheBaal Peh* – the Oral Torah. This makes this Sukkot, its offering, and its judgments uniquely different from those of the other festivals

- On sukkot, 70 bull offerings were given in atonement for the 70 nations.

- Rashi writes that their atonement by way of these offerings is connected to the judgment for rainfall.

- Sukkot is the only holiday upon which the Jews gave offerings on behalf of the nations of the world.

We see from all of these points that there is something very special and very unique about Sukkot.

Yom Kippur & Sukkot

Midrash 32:5 *And I will blot out all of the Yekum that I have made…*[7]

R' Berachya said: It means "all that exists." Rav Avun Says: It means "The inhabited world." Rabbi Levi said in the name of Reish Lakish: It refers to Kayin, who had been hanging, suspended, until the flood came and swept him away.

Bereshis Rabbah 22:13 tells us that Kayin repented before God and received a mitigated judgment. We have already seen what happened next:

> *Adam met Kayin and asked of him: "What happened? What was your judgment?" Kayin replied: "I repented and it was mitigated"*
>
> *Adam began slapping his own face and cried out: "Such is the power of repentance – and I didn't know it!" Adam immediately arose and declared:* Mizmor shir le-yom ha-Shabbat, *a Psalm, a song for the Shabbos…*

Let's look at this Midrash very carefully. It appears from this Midrash that Adam was aware of *teshuva*, repentance, but unaware of how great its power really was. When Adam saw Kayin's success in repenting, he realized something that he did not know. What was this realization? The commentaries explain:[8]

It seems that Adam was originally under the impression that *teshuvah* only helps when the sin is truly a thing of the past. If the sin is something that continues to cause harm and affect the world, then *teshuva* is ineffective. Since Adam's sin introduced death into the world, he could not repent from it. As long as people continue to die, Adam's sin continues to exert influence on the world. Therefore, from Adam's point of view, *teshuva* wasn't possible.

Applying Adam's understanding of *teshuva* to Kayin, it would seem that *teshuvah* was of no help to him either. After all, by killing Avel, Kayin prevented countless future generations from being born.

Yet, we see that Kayin was able to do *teshuva*. Why?

---

[7] Gen. 7:4.

[8] See *Beis Yitzchok* to Bereshis 7:4-5. See also the following commentaries to *Bereshis Rabbah* 32:5: Maharzu; *Eitz Yosef; Yefeh Toar* to *Bereshis Rabbah* 22:12. See Also *Matnos Kehunah*,

The answer is fascinating: God knew that there was an end in sight, a time when the effects of Kayin's sin would cease: the flood. In the flood all life, except that of one man and his family, would be destroyed. Even if Avel had descendants, they would not have survived. Since there was a time when Kayin's sin would cease to affect the world, God agreed to accept Kayin's repentance. However, it was only a partial acceptance. God would not grant atonement until the full effects of the sin were removed from the world at the time of the flood (we will discuss this point more in the live class).

Adam suddenly realized that, for him too, there was a time when his sin would cease to affect the world – the time of the World to Come. That is why Adam composed Psalm 92 – a psalm in praise of the eternal Shabbat of the world to come.

We see that the flood provided atonement for the sin of Kayin - it was, effectively, the first Day of Atonement in history. This atonement was carried out through water.

The sin of Kayin, his repentance, and the atonement of the flood is the historical anchor for Sukkot in the same way that the sin of the golden calf, the repentance of the Jews, and the atonement at Sinai is the historical anchor for Yom Kippur.

Tying it All Together

We now understand the connections between the offerings, rain, and the atonement for the nations. On Sukkot, offerings are given in the temple in atonement for the nations. Since the first atonement was brought about through water, that day also became the time for judgment of the world's water supply. The pouring of water upon the altar was part of the ceremony for securing a favorable judgment for rain. Atonement for the nations came about through the offerings of the bulls. The reason for offerings of bulls may be because the Talmud[9] tells us that the angel of rain, called Ridayah or Af Bri, appears as a bull.

---

[9] *Taanis* 25b. See also Rashi there as well as *Tosafos* to *Niddah* 16b, d.h. *Malach*. We should note that, according to *Taanis* 2a, only God decides when and where rains are to fall. The task of this angel is only to execute God's decision. See *Tosafos HaRosh* to *Nidda* ad loc.

THE YESHIVA PIRCHEI SHOSHANIM SHULCHAN ARUCH LEARNING
PROJECT

The Noahide Laws – Lesson Thirty

164 Village Path, Lakewood NJ 08701 732.370.3344
164 Rabbi Akiva, Bnei Brak, 03.616.6340

Outline of This Lesson:

1. Introduction

2. Observance of Sukkot

3. The Sukkot of Future Times

4. Sukkot Today

5. Prayers So Far...

6. Shemini Atzeres / Simchas Torah

Festivals V: Sukkot II

Introduction

As we saw in the previous lesson, Sukkot is a holiday of major importance for both Jews and Noahides. This lesson is concerned with the greater question of acknowledging this importance. How can Noahides connect with the holiday of sukkot in our times?

Observances of Sukkot

The Torah commands a number of observances to Israel on sukkot, most of which are impossible to fulfill in our times. Without the temple, we cannot perform the water libations, offerings, or many other mitzvos. Today, there are only two that remain:

> *Also in the 15th day of the seventh month, when you have gathered in the fruit of the land, you shall keep a feast to the Lord seven days; on the first day shall be a Sabbath, and on the eighth day shall be a Sabbath.* **And you shall take on the first day the boughs of goodly trees, branches of palm trees, and the boughs of thick trees, and willows of the brook; and you shall rejoice before the Lord your God seven days.** *And you shall keep it a feast to the Lord seven days in the year. It shall be a statute forever in your generations; you shall celebrate it in the seventh month.* **You shall dwell in booths seven days;** *all who are Israelites born shall dwell in booths. That your generations may know that I made the people of Israel to dwell in booths, when I brought them out of the land of Egypt; I am the Lord your God.*[1]

However, these two *mitzvos*, of taking the four species and dwelling in sukkot, were commanded only to Israel. This fact creates a problem of *chiddushei dat* for Noahides. Additionally, there are no *minhagim* (customs) for Sukkot that translate

---

[1] Lev. 23:39-43.

from Jewish to Noahide practice. In what way, then, can Noahides form a meaningful connection with the holiday of Sukkot?

The Sukkot of Future Times

Though it is clear that Noahides do not observe the Jewish mitzvos of Sukkot, this is apparently only in our times. The prophet Zechariah tells us:

> *And it shall come to pass, that every one that is left of all the nations that came against Jerusalem shall go up from year to year to worship the King, the Lord of hosts, and to keep the feast of tabernacles. And it shall be that whoever of the families of the earth that does not go up to Jerusalem to worship the King, the Lord of hosts, upon them there shall be no rain.[2]*

We see, therefore, that the nations of the world who survive the war of Gog and Magog will keep sukkot in the future, and that it will continue to be the time for judgment of water.

On a tangential note – there is a fascinating *aggadic* (non-legal or ethical) understanding of the non-Jew's future observance of sukkot brought in Avodah Zarah 3b. We will discuss it in the live class.

Sukkot Today

In much the same way that the Jews would offer sacrifices on behalf of the non-Jews of the world, taking a proactive role on their behalf, it appears that the Jewish community should take a more proactive role even now in making sukkot relatable to non-Jews.

If there is any holiday in which Noahides and Jews should come together, it is on Sukkot.

Ideally, sukkot is the time that Jews should share communal meals with Noahides in the Sukkah and that both should rejoice in their common goal: a Torah-based redemption of mankind.

However, this ideal is not as easy as it sounds. The tragic 2000-year history of Jews and Non-Jews has created a situation in which the Torah-observant community is insular and uninterested in engaging with non-Jews. It is difficult for

---

[2] Zech. 14:16-17.

30 years of Noahide interest in Torah to sway a mindset established by 2000 years of unimaginable oppression, brutality, and bloodshed. The idea of non-Jews having any positive interest in Torah is still something novel and strange to most of the Jewish world. Does the Torah-observant Jewish world trust Noahides? As a whole, the answer is "no."

This "No" must be understood in the context of history. See, for example, *Codex Judaica* by Rabbi Matis Kantor. This is an excellent year-by-year overview of Jewish history from the creation of the world until the modern era. Starting in the early middle ages, you will see that hardly a year passes without mass executions, state persecution, burnings, exile – it is a non-stop record of sorrows. Each year, tens of thousands of Jews were brutally exterminated and no one – absolutely no one – batted an eye. The world was indifferent to the Jewish oppression and suffering. As a result, the Jews had to develop a mentality that placed their own survival above all else. This mentality is still needed and still governs the Jewish attitude toward outreach. Remember, the holocaust, the last major attempted destruction of Jewry, was only 69 years ago. For the past several decades, the Jewish world has been struggling to rebuild a basis upon which their future survival can be guaranteed. All efforts are being devoted to stopping assimilation, establishing Jewish schools, encouraging mitzvos observance, and much more. In short: the Torah world today is still concerned and fighting for its own survival. The recent advent of Noahism needs more time before it can gain the necessary attention, trust, and resources trust of the mainstream Jewish world.[3]

Prayers

As with all of the holidays, the prayers are the most important part – and on Sukkot there is a LOT for which to pray.

Before getting into the prayers of Sukkot, let's do a quick review of the liturgical calendar so far:

- **1st of Elul** – We began introspection and intense self-examination in preparation for the Day of Judgment, Rosh HaShanah.

- **26th of Elul** – Noahides began saying Selichos, penitential prayers.

---

[3] Unfortunately, there are many who have lost support or become persona-non-grata in the Jewish world. To maintain support and keep an audience, they have turned to teaching Torah to Noahides, Christians, and other non-Jewish groups. Unfortunately, the fact that a Rabbi is teaching non-Jews is viewed in the Jewish world as a sign that Rabbi has lost legitimacy in his own community. This fact means that Noahides must be extremely cautious when deciding who to learn from and whose advice to accept.

- **1ˢᵗ of Tishrei, Rosh HaShanah** – Prayer and joyful evening meal with Simanim. Day prayers followed by a meal. Prayers of this day are a mixture of Joy and prayers for forgiveness.

- **From the 2ⁿᵈ of Tishrei through the seventh day of Sukkos**, it is appropriate to continue reciting Selichos. However, these Selichos are in preparation for the atonement period of Sukkot. We have provided Selichos for the four days prior to Rosh HaShanah, yet it is appropriate for Selichos to continue through the final day of Sukkot.

- **15ᵗʰ of Tishrei** – First day of Sukkot. Prayers for this period include festive meals with friends. It is appropriate for Jews to have Noahides as guests and to share meals in the Sukkah. The day time prayers of each of the Seven days include mention of the offerings of that day.

- **21ˢᵗ of Tishrei** – The final day of Sukkot. On this day, the prayer for rain is said in the congregation in the morning. The day service includes prayers for atonement. The day should be one of celebration and confidence that God will hear everyone's prayer and hearken to it.

Shemini Atzeret / Simchas Torah

The holiday of Shemini Atzeret, which falls out on the eight day after the start of Sukkot, is not part of the Sukkot holiday. Instead, it is an independent holiday.[4] The Torah discusses Shemini Atzeret in two places:

> *Seven days you shall bring an offering made by fire unto the Lord; the eighth day shall be a holy convocation to you; and you shall bring an offering made by fire unto the Lord; it is a day of solemn assembly; you shall do no manner of servile work.*[5]

And,

> *On the eighth day ye shall have a solemn assembly: ye shall do no manner of servile work.*[6]

---

[4] See Sukkot 48a.

[5] Lev. 23:36.

[6] Num. 29:35.

Curiously, though, the Torah gives no reason for this holiday.

Even the name of the holiday, *Shemini Atzeres*, yields little insight. *Shemini* means "the eighth," while the word "Atzeres," connotes "ingathering," and "assembly," as well as "holding back," and "tarrying."

The sages explain the meaning of *Shemini Atzeres* using a parable: A king throws a banquet for several days, inviting guests from all over his country. This includes his sons, who travel to be with him. At the end of the celebration, all the guests leave. However, the king asks his sons to linger, to spend one more day with him.

Similarly, the holiday of Sukkot is a seven day banquet for all the nations of the world. However, once it concludes, God asks Israel to tarry for one more day. This holiday's only purpose is to make a distinction between Israel and the non-Jewish nations. As such, it is inappropriate for Noahides to observe it.

What about *Simchas Torah*, the holiday that coincides with *Shemini Atzeres*? *Simchas Torah* is the celebration marking the renewal of the weekly cycle of Torah readings. However, there is no source for this holiday. It is not mentioned in the Torah, Talmud, or any of the foundational literature. Where does it come from?

It appears that Simchas Torah began in the 10th century. However, it was not until several hundred years later that it became universally observed in the Jewish world. Most of the customs of the holiday developed in Europe during the 14th and 15th centuries.

Is it relevant to Noahides? Possibly.

The celebration of Simchas Torah is a custom which has developed around another custom. The annual Torah cycle is also a custom developed primarily in the diaspora. In fact, it was only recently that an annual cycle has become almost universal.

THE YESHIVA PIRCHEI SHOSHANIM SHULCHAN ARUCH LEARNING PROJECT

The Noahide Laws – Lesson Thirty One

Outline of This Lesson:

1. Introduction

2. Cheshvan / MarCheshvan

3. Kislev

4. The Timeline of the Flood

5. Curious Things...

6. The Meaning of a Rainbow

7. The Noahide Covenant vs. The Noahide Laws

8. The First of Kislev

Festivals VI: Cheshvan & Kislev

Introduction

Following Sukkot and the conclusion of the month of Tishrei, we enter the months of Cheshvan and Kislev. Cheshvan contains no holidays, yet its relationship to Kislev is important for reasons that we shall see.

Cheshvan / MarCheshvan

The 2nd month of the new year (and 8th month over all) is Cheshvan. Cheshvan is commonly referred to as *Marcheshvan*, which literally means "bitter Cheshvan." Why is this month called bitter? One reason is because it is the only month with no holidays. Another is that a number of tragic events happened to Israel in this month. For example, on the 5th of Cheshvan the Chaldeans murdered the sons of king Tzidkiyahu, blinded him, and took him into captivity. On the 15th of Cheshvan Yarovam ben Nevat aroused God's wrath against Israel.

However, *mar* may also refer to the flood of Noah. According to most chronologies of the flood, the rains began on the 28th or 27th of Cheshvan. Curiously, Cheshvan is called *Bul* in Melachim I 6:8. Many commentaries explain that this term *Bul* is derived from the word *mabul*, which means flood. *Mar* can also mean "a drop of water," as we see from Isaiah 40:15. Of course, Cheshvan is also the start of the rainy season in Israel, and *mar*, meaning "drop," may be an indication of this quality.

Kislev

The month of Kislev follow Cheshvan. Kislev is famously known for the holiday of Chanukah. Beginning on the 25th of Kislev, Chanukah commemorates the Jewish victory over the Seleucid Greeks and the miracles wrought for Israel in their fight for religious freedom.

Given that Chanukah is an entirely rabbinic holiday commemorating a Jewish victory, it has no relevance to Noahides and should not be observed. However there is a major historical event that occurred in Kislev which is of extreme importance to Noahides.

The Timeline of the Flood

It is very difficult to pin down the exact chronology of the events of the flood. Nevertheless, most commentaries agree that it began at the end of Cheshvan (on the 27th or 28th of that month) and ended one year later, with Noah emerging from the Ark on the 28th of Cheshvan.

Upon Noah's exit from the Ark, he had much to do:

> *And Noach built an altar to God. He took from all of the pure animals and all of the pure fowl and he sacrificed burnt-offerings upon the altar.*[1]

It was only after these offerings that God was appeased:

> *And the Lord smelled the sweet savor, and the Lord said in His heart: "I will not again curse the ground any more on account of man; for the thoughts of man's heart is evil from his youth,*[2] *neither will I again smite any more everything living, as I have done.*[3]

Upon making this decision, God blessed Noah and his family, and stuck a new covenant with mankind:

> *And God blessed Noah and his sons, and said unto them: 'Be fruitful and multiply, and replenish the earth. And the fear of you and the dread of you shall be upon every beast of the earth, and upon every fowl of the air, and upon all that teems on the ground, and upon all the fish of the sea: into your hand are they delivered. Every moving thing that lives shall be for food for you; as the green herb have I given you all.*[4]

---

[1] Gen. 8:20.

[2] This curious statement will be discussed below.

[3] Gen. 8:21.

[4] Gen. 9:1-3.

At this point, God completed the commanding of the Noahide laws with the seventh and final commandment:[5]

> *Only flesh with the life thereof, which is the blood thereof, shall ye not eat.*[6]

God then gave mankind a sign of this covenant:

> *And God spoke unto Noah, and to his sons with him, saying: 'As for Me, behold, I establish My covenant with you, and with your seed after you; and with every living creature that is with you, the fowl, the cattle, and every beast of the earth with you; of all that go out of the ark, even every beast of the earth. And I will establish My covenant with you; neither shall all flesh be cut off any more by the waters of the flood; neither shall there again be a flood to destroy the earth.' And God said: 'This is the token of the covenant which I make between Me and you and every living creature that is with you, for perpetual generations: I have set My bow in the cloud, and it shall be for a token of a covenant between Me and the earth. And it shall come to pass, when I bring clouds over the earth, and the bow is seen in the cloud, that I will remember My covenant, which is between Me and you and every living creature of all flesh; and the waters shall no more become a flood to destroy all flesh. And the bow shall be in the cloud; and I will look upon it, that I may remember the everlasting covenant between God and every living creature of all flesh that is upon the earth.' And God said unto Noah: 'This is the token of the covenant which I have established between Me and all flesh that is upon the earth.'*[7]

When did all of this occur? According to most commentaries, it couldn't have been on the 28th of Cheshvan, the day that Noah emerged from the ark. The building of the altar and preparations for the sacrifices would have taken at least a few days. Therefore, the covenant of the rainbow was most likely given on or shortly after the first day of Kislev.[8]

---

[5] This is according to Maimonides in _Hilchos Melachim_ 9:1. Tosafos, as mentioned in a prior lesson, however, holds that all seven were commanded to Adam. In the times of Noah the details of the seven _mitzvos_ were only modified and reaffirmed. Either way, this covenant marks an important point in the commanding of the Noahide laws.

[6] Gen. 9:4.

[7] Gen. 9:8-17.

[8] See _Sefer Todaah_, _hakdama_ to Kislev.

Curious Things...

The events surrounding Noah's exit from the ark are riddled with mysteries. Particularly striking is this passage:

> *And the Lord smelled the sweet savor, and the Lord said in His heart: "I will not again curse the ground any more on account of man;* **for the thoughts of man's heart are evil from his youth**,[9] *neither will I again smite any more everything living, as I have done.*[10]

This passage seems to state that, because man is inherently evil, he not culpable for his actions. At a minimum, culpability for his actions is not at such a level so as to warrant destruction of the earth. Yet, this cannot be the correct understanding of this passage. Consider what is written before the flood:

> *And the Lord saw that the wickedness of man was great upon the earth,* **and that every impulse of the thoughts of his heart was evil, always**.[11]

The "evil in man's heart" cannot be both the reason for bringing the flood (as stated before the flood) and the justification for never again bringing a flood (as stated after the flood)!

The relationship of these two verses is one of the most difficult concepts to understand in the Torah, and many commentaries have wrestled with it. To be clear, there are two issues at play:

1) What does it mean that "… every impulse of the thoughts of his heart was evil, always?" Is man inherently evil? It is a difficult proposition to entertain in light of everything else that we have learned. And,

2) How do we resolve the first use of this phrase (pre-flood) against the second (post-flood)?

A particularly attractive interpretation of these two questions is offered by the *Bina Le-Ittim*.[12]

---

[9] This curious statement will be discussed below.

[10] Gen. 8:21.

[11] Genesis 6:5.

[12] Cited in R' Yehudah Nachshoni's *Hagos B'Parshios HaTorah* on *Parshas Noah*.

The Torah writes:

> *And God saw everything that He had made, and, behold, it was very good.*[13]

The Midrash explains:

> *R' Nachamn bar Shmuel bar Nachman said in the name of Rav Shmuel bar Nachman: … "And, behold, it was very good." This refers to the evil inclination. But, is the evil inclination "very good?" If not for the evil inclination, man would never build a house, take a wife, reproduce, or conduct any business. So too said Solomon: "[And I saw that all labor and all skillful enterprise] spring from man's rivalry with his neighbor."*[14]

When the Torah states that …*for the thoughts of man's heart are evil from his youth,* and … *that every impulse of the thoughts of his heart was evil, always,* it is referring to man's evil inclination, the *yetzer ha-ra.*

Before the flood, the world only used the *yetzer ha-ra* for evil. Its desires were only to be indulged and enjoyed. After the flood though, when Noah offered his offerings to God, God saw that the *yetzer ha-ra* was once again being used as a tool for good. This is why, before the flood, God criticizes man for his *yetzer ha-ra.* After the flood, however, the reference to the desires of man's heart is actually in praise of man.

What, though, does it mean that Noah, in offering the sacrifices, was using his *yetzer ha-ra* for good? We will discuss this further in our live class.

The Meaning of a Rainbow

God's choice of a rainbow as the sign of his renewed covenant with man has been the subject of many interpretations, some of which are more fanciful and creative than others. Here is an anthology of the approaches of the classical scholars of the Torah:

- **Talmud** <u>Chagigah 16a</u> - *Anyone who does not care about his Creator's honor, it would be merciful for him had he not been created. In other words, better off that this person was never created. Who is such a person? Rabbi Abba says this is one who stares at a rainbow. As it says, 'Like the appearance of the rainbow that will be in the clouds on a rainy day, so was the appearance of the brilliance all around.' (Ezek. 1:28) That was the appearance of the similitude of God's honor'."* According to this *gemara,* God's presence is manifested somehow in the appearance of a rainbow. Just as one may not

---

[13] Gen. 1:31.

[14] Ecc. 4:4.

stare at any manifestation of the *shechina*, the divine presence, so too one may not stare at a rainbow. To do so is to slight God's honor. This passage also tells us that staring at a rainbow damages one's sight.

- *Bereshis Rabbah* **35:2 & Kesubos 77b** – When Eliyahu HaNavi was studying Torah with Rabbi Yehoshua ben Levi, they encountered a difficulty in a statement of Rabbi Shimon bar Yochai, the author of the Zohar. Since Rabbi Shimon bar Yochai was no longer living, the two of them ascended to *Gan Eden* to ask Rabbi Shimon for clarification of his words. Eliyahu approached Rabbi Shimon first. Rabbi Shimon asked him: "Who is this with you?" Eliyahu HaNavi answered: "Rabbi Yehoshua ben Levi, one of the great ones of his generation." Rabbi Shimon turned to Rabbi Yehoshua and asked: "Has a rainbow ever been seen in your generation?" Rabbi Yehoshua answered: "yes," to which Rabbi Shimon replied: "If a rainbow has been seen in your generation, then you are not fit to learn from me!" The commentaries explain that the fact that a rainbow had appeared in Rabbi Yehoshua's generation indicated that his generation was worthy of destruction. Therefore, Rabbi Yehoshua was not of sufficient righteousness or purity to speak to the holy Rabbi Shimon. The *gemora* in Kesubos 77b, however, tells us that a rainbow never appeared in the generation of Rabbi Yehoshua. Why then did Rabbi Yehoshua tell Rabbi Shimon that a rainbow had appeared? The *gemora* explains that Rabbi Yehoshua did not want to be seen as haughty.

- Rashi **to Gen. 9:14** – Based on the Midrash, Rashi explains that when God desires to bring punishment upon the world, he places the rainbow as a sign of the covenant, as a reminder that He will not destroy the world. Therefore, the appearance of a rainbow is not a good sign. Rather, it is a sign that things are not right between God and the world and, were it not for the covenant, God would again destroy the world! In fact, the *Mishnah Berurah*,[15] the most widely accepted interpretation of the Shulchan Aruch today, states that if one sees a rainbow, even though it is something upon which we bless, one should not inform others because it is not a good sign.

- Nachmanides **(the Ramban)** – The Rainbow appears like a bow without a string. Instead of aimed from heaven downwards, it is upturned, away from the earth. This symbolizes that God does not "hold destruction over the earth." Furthermore, the unstrung bow is a sign of peace. The Ramban further writes that we see that rainbows are a natural phenomenon caused by water refracted through moisture. Therefore, they must have existed since the

---

[15] 229:1.

beginning of creation. It was only after the flood that a particular meaning was assigned to the rainbow. This is implied by the verse's wording: "I have **set** my rainbow…," implying that the rainbow already existed. This is also the opinion of Rav Saadya Gaon.

- **Ibn Ezra & Radak** – The rainbow did not exist prior to the flood.

- **Chizkuni** – The appearance of opposite colors together symbolized a resolution of opposite ends. Blue against red, for example symbolized the resolution of fire and water, of mercy and harsh judgment.

- **Rav Shimshon Rafael Hirsch** – Rav Hirsch, an exceedingly deep thinker of 19th century Judaism, offered the following interpretation of the rainbow:[16]

Perhaps, the appearance of the rainbow's colors is closest in meaning [to the actual meaning of the rainbow] than all these aforementioned interpretations. By it, our attention is repeatedly drawn to the fact that, despite all the variances in the degrees of the development of mankind, God would never again decree the downfall of the entire human race. Rather, the differences and varieties found among humanity would serve as the basis for mankind's gradual education towards its godly purpose. For the rainbow is nothing other than a single, pure ray of light broken into seven degrees of seven colors. [It ranges] from the red rays nearest to the light to violet – the most distant from the light and the nearest to darkness. Yet, from one to the other, are they not all but rays of light, and do they not all combine to form a single, pure, white ray? Could this not, perhaps, be intended to say that the whole array of living creatures, from Adam, the most alive and whose name means "red one," the nearest to God, all the way down to the lowest, humblest worm in whom there is a living soul of flesh, and even moreso all of the variety and shades of humanity among the races of mankind – from the brilliant intellectuals to those in whom there is hardly a glimmer of the spiritual - that God unites them all in a common bond of peace. All are fragments of one life; all are refracted rays of the one spirit of God. [Is not] the lowest, darkest, most distant one not still a son of the light? Thus we see later on that our sages describe the different spiritual and moral degrees of the righteous using the metaphor of degrees of light; from the bright illuminating rays of the sun to the gleam of the menorah in the temple. All is light, yet it only appears different according to the difference of the material, [as it is written:] "There are seven groups among the righteous… and their faces shine like the sun,[17] like the moon,[18] like the firmament,[19] like lightening,[20] like the stars,[21] like the blossoms,[22] and like the menorah[23] in the holy temple."[24]

---

[16] Commentary of Rav Hirsch to Gen. 9:16. Editor's translation from the original German.

[17] See Song of Songs 6:10.

It is important to note that all of the above interpretations embody that quality that we have seen so many times in this course: paradox. The rainbow, a sign of peace, potential, and resolution, is also a sign of warning and displeasure. These apparent opposites both exist simultaneously, underscoring the complex relationship between God and his creation. God is both merciful father and true judge, the immanent and the transcendent, the destroyer and creator, the giver of life and one who decrees death, the God of light, dark, and all of the colors in-between. Perhaps, the expression of this complicated paradox is part of the full meaning of the rainbow.

For Jews, Kislev is deeply connected with Chanukah, a commemoration of the triumph of Torah over the onslaught of Greek thought and subjugation. For Noahides, Kislev is associated with the original Noahic covenant. Should this association be commemorated? May a Noahide celebrate the 1st of Kislev as a commemoration of the original covenant?

The Noahide Covenant vs. The Noahide Laws

We must make a careful distinction as to what the first of Kislev commemorates. It was on or about the first of Kislev that God gave man permission to eat meat, blessed Noah and his sons, and guaranteed that He would no longer destroy the world on account of man.

However, it is not a commemoration of the giving of the Noahide laws. Even though the Noahide laws were completed (or modified to their final form, according to some)[25] at this time, their binding authority today is from Sinai, not from the covenant with Noah. It is not appropriate to commemorate the first of Kislev as a time of the giving of the Noahide laws – that honor belongs to

---

[18] Ibid.

[19] Dan. 12:3.

[20] Nahum 2:5.

[21] Dan. 12:3.

[22] A poetic reference to the prophets. See Psalm 69:1.

[23] Zech. 4:2.

[24] This statement shows up in many places. See *Midrash Tehillim* 16:12; *Pseikta d'Rav Kehana*, 27:2.

[25] See note 5, above.

Shavuot, the commemoration of the revelation at Sinai. Recall that Sinai is the basis for modern observance of the Noahide laws, not the Noahic covenant.

The First of Kislev

If one wishes, he may commemorate the 1st of Kislev as an historical milestone. However, one should keep in mind that the day is of limited religious significance; its primary religious significance was supplanted by the events at Sinai. Nevertheless, it is appropriate to recall the rainbow as a sign of God's promise and to pray that all man will return to God.

THE YESHIVA PIRCHEI SHOSHANIM SHULCHAN ARUCH LEARNING PROJECT

The Noahide Laws – Lesson Thirty Two

164 Village Path, Lakewood NJ 08701 732.370.3344
164 Rabbi Akiva, Bnei Brak, 03.616.6340

Outline of This Lesson:

1. Introduction

2. *Tu B'Shvat*: The New Year For Trees

3. *Tu B'Shvat, Terumos & Maasros*

4. *Tu B'Shvat, Orlah, Neta Reavi*

5. Are *Terumos & Maasros* Relevant to Noahides?

6. Maimonides

7. An Ongoing Dispute?

8. Jewish Commemoration of *Tu B'Shvat*

9. The Evolution of a Custom

Festivals VII: Tu B'Shvat

Lesson

32

Introduction

Shvat is the month that follows Kislev. The only holiday occurring in this month is *Tu B'Shvat*. However, there is some uncertainty as to whether or not this day is relevant to Noahides. Exploring this question will be the main topic of our lesson.

Tu B'Shvat: The New Year for Trees

The Mishnah[1] teaches us:

> *There are four* Rosh Hashanahs *[New Years]: the 1ˢᵗ of Nissan is the New Year for kings and festivals, the 15ᵗʰ of Elul is the New Year for the tithing of animals (according to Rabbis Elazar and Shimon, this is on the 1ˢᵗ of Tishrei), the 1ˢᵗ of Tishrei for counting years, the Jubilee and Shemitta cycles, and the tithing of trees and produce. The 1ˢᵗ of Shvat is the New Year for trees according to the yeshiva [school] of Shammai.* **According to the yeshiva [school] of Hillel, it is on the 15ᵗʰ of Shvat.**

Since the *halakhah*, practice, always follows Hillel,[2] then we see that *Tu B'Shvat* is established on the 15ᵗʰ of Shvat. In fact, the name "Tu B'Shvat" literally means "the 15ᵗʰ of Shvat."

---

[1] *Rosh HaShanah 1:1.*

[2] There are, however, six exceptions to this rule in the Talmudic canon.

Tu B'Shvat, Terumos & Maasros

A number of standard agricultural tithes were given each year in ancient Israel. There were also variable tithes dependent on the seven year *shemitta* cycle. The cycle was as follows:

- **Year 1** – *Terumah Gedolah, Maaser Rishon* (and *Terumas HaMaaser*) & *Maaser Sheni*

- **Year 2** – *Terumah Gedolah, Maaser Rishon* (and *Terumas HaMaaser*) & *Maaser Sheni*

- **Year 3** – *Terumah Gedolah, Maaser Rishon* (and *Terumas HaMaaser*) & *Maaser Ani*

- **Year 4** – *Terumah Gedolah, Maaser Rishon* (and *Terumas HaMaaser*) & *Maaser Sheni*

- **Year 5** – *Terumah Gedolah, Maaser Rishon* (and *Terumas HaMaaser*) & *Maaser Sheni*

- **Year 6** – *Terumah Gedolah, Maaser Rishon* (and *Terumas HaMaaser*) & *Maaser Ani*

- **Year 7** – *Shemitta Year.* Land may not be worked; Remission of debts.

Terumah Gedolah – This was the first separation and was given to the *Kohanim,* [**Priests**] of the temple. The minimum amount of this tithe varied depending on whether the owner of the produce was poor or wealthy.

Maaser Rishon – A tithe of $1/10^{th}$ removed after *Terumah Gedolah.* This was gifted to the Levites.

Terumas HaMasser – From the *Maaser Rishon* they received, the Levites were obligated to give $1/10^{th}$ to the *Kohanim.* This amounts to $1/100^{th}$ of the total produce.

Maaser Sheni – This tithe (another $1/10^{th}$ of the remaining produce) was separated only in the 1st, 2nd, 4th, and 5th years of the *shemitta* cycle.

Maaser Ani – This tithe, given to the poor, was given only in the 3rd and 6th years of the *shemitta* cycle.

An important part of these laws was the rule that one may not satisfy the tithing obligation of one year with the fruit produced in another year. For fruit trees, *Tu B'Shvat* marks the demarcation line between one year and the next for the purposes of these tithes.

Tu B'shvat, Orlah & Neta Revai

Tu B'Shvat is also important for two further *mitzvos*: *Orlah* and *Neta Revai*.

- **Orlah** – One may not eat fruit yielded by a tree in its first three years. While the start of this three-year period is based on the 1st of Tishrei, the end of this period is after the *Tu B'Shvat* of the third year of the tree's life. For example, if one planted trees before Rosh HaShanah, the fruit of those trees would be prohibited until after the third *Tu B'Shvat* after the Tree was planted.

- **Neta Revai** – Fruit produced by a tree in its fourth year is similar to *Maaser Sheni*; it may only be consumed in Jerusalem. Alternatively, one may redeem this produce and use the money to buy food to consume in Jerusalem. *Tu B'Shvat* is also used to calculate the fourth year for *Neta Revai*.

Are *Terumos* and *Maasros* Relevant to Noahides?

It is clear that Noahides are not obligated in *Terumos* and *Maasros*. This is the universal conclusion of the *halachic* authorities.[3] After all, these *mitzvos* were commanded only to Jews. Therefore, Noahide performance of these *mitzvos* can only be voluntary at best.

The Mishnah[4] certainly implies this, stating that such a voluntary tithing is valid:

---

[3] See Rambam 4:15; Ridvaz ad loc; Sefer Mitzvos HaShem (Shteif), Mitzvos Bnei Noach. This is also the implication of the Mishnah, as we shall see.

[4] Terumos 3:9.

> *The Terumah of a non-Jew or Cuthean is Terumah, their tithes are valid tithes, and their sanctified gifts are sanctified gifts.*

However, there is significant doubt as to whether or not the validity of these separations is biblical or rabbinic in nature. If it is biblical, then *Tu B'Shvat* is a significant date for Noahides. However, if it is rabbinic, then *Tu B'Shvat* might not be relevant to Noahides.

Most authorities appear to hold that the validity of a Noahides voluntary separations is only rabbinic. However, things are not so clear.

Maimonides

In his Mishnah Torah,[5] Maimonides explains the reason for the rabbinic decree:

> *When a gentile separates Terumah from his own produce, according to Biblical Law, the separation is ineffective because he has no obligation to do so. [Our Rabbis] decreed that his separation should be effective, though, because of the wealthy, lest the money belong to a Jew and he say that it belong to a gentile to make it exempt. We cross-examine the gentile who separates Terumah. If he says: "I separated it so that it should be like a Jew's," we give it to a priest. If not, it should be entombed, for perhaps his intent was [to dedicate it] to heaven. When does the above apply? In Eretz Yisrael. Our Sages did not, however, issue a decree if a gentile separates Terumah in the Diaspora. We tell him that he is not obligated to do this and the produce is not Terumah at all.*

According to what is written here, the tithes of a non-Jew are only acceptable in the Temple because of a rabbinic decree made to address a problem in the Jewish world. Apparently, wealthy people would occasionally falsify ownership of their crops and produce, claiming they belonged to a non-Jew, in order to escape paying the regular, obligated tithes. If a non-Jew came to voluntarily offer tithes, there was suspicion that it may be a ruse.

While this passage implies that Maimonides holds of only rabbinic validity to these tithes, this is not definite.

Maimonides, commenting on our aforementioned Mishnah from Terumos 3:9, writes:

> *Non-Jews, even though they are not obligated in these separations or tithes, they receive a little benefit by giving them… therefore they are valid.[6]*

---

[5] Terumos 4:15.

[6] Peirush al Hamishnayos.

This remark certainly implies that, though not obligated in *Terumos* and *Maasros*, non-Jews may separate these tithes and they are accorded a *mitzvah* for doing so. It appears that Maimonides acknowledges the biblical validity of these tithes.

An Ongoing Dispute?

Tosafos to Kiddushin 41b implies that this question may be an ongoing Talmudic dispute. There are a number of possibilities as to how we can understand the relationship of the texts involved.[7]

1) The Mishnah is saying the same thing as Maimonides, that the tithes and separations of non-Jews are only valid per force of Rabbinic decree. The disagreement in the Talmud, however, is only relevant to determining whether or not the validity of a non-Jew's *Terumah* is comparable to a Jew's for the purpose of acting as a Jew's agent in separating these tithes. It is not directly relevant to whether or not non-Jews can validly separate *Terumah* and *Maaser*.

2) The Mishnah states that, on a biblical level, the separation of *Terumah* and *Maaser* by a non-Jew is valid. Maimonides agrees to this (as we see in his commentary on the Mishnah). However, in the Mishnah Torah Maimonides is only addressing the issue from the "Jewish side" of things; in a situation of doubt caused by possibile dishonesty. We cannot determine anything about the validity of a true Noahide separation of *Maaser* or *Terumah* from what Maimonides writes there. The Talmud in Kiddushin may not be relevant for the same reason mentioned earlier – it is only discussing validity for the purposes of agency.

So, what is the conclusion? Are the voluntary *Terumos* and *Maasros* of a non-Jew valid because of the rabbinic decree mentioned by the Rambam, or is because they are intrinsically valid? There isn't a clear answer. Yet, this isn't the end of things…

---

[7] See Toldos Noach 13:10.

Jewish Commemoration of *Tu B'Shvat*

How do Jews commemorate *Tu B'Shvat*? Many have the custom to plant trees on this day. However, this custom is very recent. It only began in 1890 in Zichron Yaakov, an agricultural commune in pre-state Israel. The practice was adopted in the early 1900's by a number of early religious Zionist movements has since become prevalent in the Reform and Conservative movements.

Traditionally, Tu B'Shvat was not celebrated as a holiday. Other than omitting certain supplications from the regular liturgy, there are no assigned commemorations for this holiday.

However, in the middle ages some began to acknowledge the day with a quasi-ceremonial eating-of-fruit. The origin of this custom seems to come from Rashi's commentary to *Rosh HaShanah* 14a. Rashi comes to answer an obvious question: Why is the 15th of Shvat the New Year for trees and not some other day? Though the Talmud loosely connects *Tu B'Shvat* to the lifecycle of fruit trees, Rashi makes things much clearer for us. According to Rashi, *Tu B'Shvat* is the day on which an internal process begins within the tress of the world. On this day, they begin to draw their sap up from the roots to nourish the tree through the winter season. Botanically, this marks the renewal of the lifecycle of the tree - a cycle eventually culminating in fruit. Today, when the *Trumah* and *Maaser* cycle is mostly inapplicable,[8] it would seem that that this quasi-ceremonial fruit eating is an acknowledgement of the physical process taking place in the world on Tu B'Shvat.

The Evolution of a Custom

Over the next few hundred years, the custom of eating fruit on this day became more commonplace and widespread. The ceremony also became more elaborate, eventually culminating in a standardized Seder. The form of this ceremony was fixed by the Ari Za"l and his students, in whose hands the custom took on deep mystical significance.

I numerous places, man is compared to a tree. For example, Deut. 20:19 states:

When you besiege a city for many days to wage war against it to capture it, you shall not destroy its trees by wielding an ax against them, for you may eat from them, but you shall not cut them down. Is the tree of the field a man, to go into the siege before you?

---

[8] In the land of Israel, there are some remaining, residual requirements of tithing. However, they are not given to Kohanim in our days.

The language of this verse is such that it can be read as saying "A man is but a tree of the field…" From here the Talmud draws a number of comparisons between a man and a tree.[9] Jeremiah 17:8 also compares a righteous person to a tree planted by water. Such comparisons are also common in the Psalms, Midrashim, and other sources.

The Ari Za"l and his school explained that these comparisons are far more than parables or literary devices. On a very deep level, they allude to the connection between the soul of Adam, both as the first man and as all of mankind, and the original tree – the Tree of Knowledge.

Their *Seder* for this meal invokes themes of restoring and repairing the spiritual damages caused by man's very early transgressions.

From a perspective of Torah law, the Noahide relationship to *Tu B'Shvat* is only to the degree that voluntary *Terumah* and *Maaser* may be brought according to the agricultural calendar. However, from a perspective of natural phenomena (see Rashi's opinion above) and kabbalah, there is certainly enough connection to warrant commemoration of the holiday using the Ari's *Seder*.

Yeshiva Pirchei Shoshanim has prepared a translated and annotated edition of the Ari Zt"l's *Seder* for *Tu B'Shvat*. We have included it with this lesson.

---

[9] See Taanis 7a.

The Noahide Laws – Lesson Thirty Three

164 Village Path, Lakewood NJ 08701 732.370.3344
164 Rabbi Akiva, Bnei Brak, 03.616.6340

Table of Contents:

1. Introduction

2. 7th of Adar

3. Month of Nissan

4. Nissan as the Rosh HaShanah for Kings and Festivals

5. New Year for Kings

6. Judgment for Grain

7. *Birkas Hallanos* – Blessing on the Trees

8. *Birkas HaChama* – The Blessing on the Cycle of the Sun

9. Summary

Adar & Nissan

Introduction

The next month in the calendar is Adar. The only major holiday in Adar is Purim, a Rabbinic celebration commemorating the victory of the Jews over their Persian oppressors. Like Chanukah, this day is of little significance to Noahides. However, there are other days, though not as well-known as Purim, that are nevertheless significant. In this lesson, we will also look at the month of Nissan and the holiday of Passover.

The 7th of Adar

The 7th of Adar is the anniversary of both Moses's birth and death. Though are no special commemorations for this day, there are a number of customs that have grown up around it. However, most of these customs are not universally observed. In the past, there were some who had the custom to fast on the 7th of Adar and to recite a special prayer. However, this is uncommon in our days. There are some who light a *yahrzeit* (memorial) candle in memory of Moses. In many communities, Jewish burial societies hold their annual meetings on the 7th of Adar.

For Noahides, Moses is a significant figure in the transmission of the Noahide laws and it is certainly important to acknowledge his role. The 7th of Adar is the appropriate day to do so.

- As a general rule, fasting is discouraged unless one has a particularly compelling reason to do so. Nevertheless, one may still recite the prayer for the 7th of Adar (this will be provided to the group in the near future).

- Lighting a 24-hour memorial candle in memory of Moses is an appropriate custom.

This year the 7th of Adar is Thursday, February 26. 2015.

In a Hebrew leap year, when there is an extra month of Adar, the 7th of Adar is commemorated in Adar II.

The Month of Nissan

The Month of Nissan is second only to Tishrei in religious significance. As with all of the major festivals of the Torah, it has levels of specific meaning relevant only to Israel and broader meaning relevant to the world. Let's take a look again at our source Mishnah's:

> *There are four* Rosh Hashanah's *[New Years]:* **the 1st of Nissan is the New Year for kings and festivals**, *the 15th of Elul is the New Year for the tithing of animals (according to Rabbis Elazar and Shimon, this is on the 1st of Tishrei), the 1st of Tishrei for counting years, the Jubilee and Shemitta cycles, and the tithing of trees and produce. The 1st of Shvat is the New Year for trees according to the yeshiva [school] of Shammai. According to the yeshiva [school] of Hillel, it is on the 15th of Shvat.*[1]

> *At four junctures, the world is judged:* **on Passover for grain**, *on Shavuot for fruits, on Rosh Hashanah all pass before him like sheep of the flock, as it is written, "He form their hearts as one, he understands all of their deeds." (Psalms 33). On Sukkot, the world is judged for water.*[2]

For Jews, the Month of Nissan is all about Passover, the liberation of Israel from the slavery of Egypt. However, the universal meaning is two-fold:

1) The 1st of Nissan is a Rosh HaShanah for Kings and festivals.

2) On the 15th of Nissan, Passover, the world is judged upon the abundance of grain.

---

[1] Mishnah Rosh HaShanah 1:1.

[2] Mishnah Rosh HaShanah 1:2.

Nissan as the Rosh HaShanah for Kings and Festivals

Before Israel exited Egypt, the months of the Hebrew calendar were all counted from varying starting points. Either the months were counted from creation, from the cessation of the flood, or the birth of Abraham. After the exodus, however, God commanded Israel to count all of the months beginning from Nissan:

> *And the Lord spoke unto Moses and Aaron in the land of Egypt, saying: "This month shall be unto you the beginning of months; it shall be the first month of the year to you." (Exodus 12:1-2)*

Having established Nissan as the first month, Pesach (Passover) is thus reckoned as the first of the festivals. This is important for calculating the window one has to fulfill a vows pertaining to offering (this detail will be discussed in the live class). This aspect of Nissan may be relevant to Noahides and will be discussed in greater detail in a future lesson.

This year, the first of Nissan falls on Saturday, March 21, 2015.

The New Year for Kings

The Talmud clarifies that Nissan is only considered the New Year for the reign of Jewish kings. This is because of the unique status of Nissan for Jews as the month of Redemption. For gentile kings, their reign is counted from the time of creation, the month of Tishrei.

We see that the status of Tishrei as a Rosh HaShanah for kings is only relevant to Jews. Yet, as a Rosh HaShanah for festivals, it may be relevant to Noahides.

Judgment for Grain

The 15th of Nissan is Passover for the Jews – a holiday primarily concerned with commemorating the exodus from Egypt. For the rest of the world, its primary relevance is as a day of judgment for grain.

It is on this day that God determines which nations will prosper and which will have famine. As such, it is important to pray for the sustenance of the world at this time.

On Passover, we also recite the prayer for dew. The reason for this prayer is that the rains that fall after the 15th of Nissan are damaging for the grain harvest. An excess of moisture at this time can cause the drying grain to rot. Therefore, on the 15th of Nissan we pray for dew, asking God for a sufficient amount of moisture to sustain the crops and the world without harming the drying grain. This prayer is recited on the first day of Passover during morning prayers.

Communal are certainly appropriate at this time. It is also appropriate to eat bread and food from grains at this meal.

For Noahides, the 15th of Nissan is a one-day holiday. This year it falls on Saturday, April 4, 2015.

Birkas Hallanos – Blessing on the Trees

Nissan is strongly associated with spring, renewal, and the emergence of the world from its winter slumber. During this month, upon seeing fruit trees in bloom, we make a special blessing upon them. This blessing may be made only once each year. Some have the custom to gather in groups, making the occasion one for celebration. This blessing is subject to the following rules:

- The blessing is said only upon fruit bearing trees. It a dispute as to whether or not this blessing may be said in any month other than Nissan.

- The blessing is only recited when one sees at least two fruit bearing trees together. These trees should be over 3 years old.

- According to some, this blessing should not be made on the seventh day or on a holiday.

- If one has already seen blossoming trees, then the blessing is not recited.

- The blessing is not recited upon a tree that is actually laden with fruit, only upon a tree that is blossoming.

This is the blessing on blossoming fruit trees:

Blessed are You, Lord, our God, King of the Universe, in Whose universe nothing is lacking, and in which He created good creatures and good trees, in which mankind takes joy.

Birkas HaChama – The Blessing on the Cycle of the Sun

The Blessing on the Sun is a blessing recited once every 28 years. Due to its infrequency, this blessing has become a special occasion for rejoicing. The Talmud writes:

> *One who sees the sun at the beginning of its cycle … recites: Blessed in the One who makes the creation. And when is this? Abaye said: Every 28 years.*[3]

Conventional wisdom, that the sun rises in the east and sets in the west, is only mostly true. The exact positions of its rising and setting vary from season-to-season. Near the summer solstice, the sun rises and sets at its northernmost point. However, near the winter solstice, the sun's rising and setting is at its southernmost place. The midpoint of the sun's southern journey is the autumnal equinox, while the midpoint of its northern journey is the spring equinox. The interval between the reoccurrence of these phases is the solar year, which is approximately 365 ¼ days, or 52 weeks and 1 ¼ day.

Due to the additional 1 ¼ day, these solar benchmarks shift forward slightly each year. For example, if the spring equinox is at 12:00 PM on a Sunday, then it will fall on Monday at 6:00 PM in the following year. The next year, it will fall at midnight on Tuesday, and so on.

After 28 years will the sun have returned back to its original position at the same time we began our count.

The sun was placed in the heavens during the first hour on the evening of the fourth day of the week (a Tuesday night).[4] According to the sages, this was the Spring Equinox. Therefore, the first sunrise occurred twelve hours later on the morning of the fourth day. It is at that time, every 28 years that we make the blessing on the sun.

2009 was the last time that the blessing was made. The next occasion for this blessing is April 8, 2037.

---

[3] Brachos 59b.

[4] The details here are all summarized from Brachos 2a & 59b, Eruvin 56a, Rosh HaShanah 10b.

This blessing is recited according to the following laws:

- The blessing is cited as soon as the entire disk of the sun has risen above the horizon.

- The blessing may only be said until the third hour of daylight. According to some, if one misses that time, then he may recite it until noon.

- It is preferable that this blessing be recited by as many people together as possible.

- Women do not recite this blessing. This is because, in the times of the Prophet Jeremiah, worship of the sun became widespread among women of the time.

- It is customary for the congregation to assemble before sunrise for their prayers, timing them so that they have ample time afterwards to make the blessing.

- Following the blessing, the custom is to celebrate with song, music, and food.

The blessing is:

Blessed are You, Lord our God, who makes the work of Creation.

Summary of the Lesson

1. Nissan, as a Rosh HaShanah may be relevant to Noahides because it established the window of time during which one must fulfill a vow to bring a voluntary offering.

2. Nissan, as a Rosh HaShanah for kings, is not relevant to Noahides

3. The 15th of Nissan is important as a day of judgment for grain and produce.

4. On the 15th of Nissan we recite the prayer for dew.

5. During Nissan, we recite the blessing on blooming fruit trees.

6. Every 28 years, we make a blessing upon God's renewal of the cycle of the sun.

The Noahide Laws - Lesson Thirty Four

164 Village Path, Lakewood NJ 08701 732.370.3344
164 Rabbi Akiva, Bnei Brak, 03.616.6340

Table of Contents:

1. Introduction

2. The Noahide Covenant & Man

3. Judgment on the Fruit of the Trees

4. Observances for *Shavuos*

5. *Tisha B'Av* – the 8th of Av

6. Jewish Observances of *Tisha B'Av*

7. *Tisha B'Av* & Noahides – Mourning the Temples

8. Summary

Sivan & Av

Lesson

34

Introduction

The next important holiday is _Shavuos,_ which is on the 6th of Sivan. For Jews, _Shavuos_ is primarily the _zman matan Torosaynu_ – the time of the giving of the Torah. However, for Noahides it carries a different yet equally important connotation. In this lesson we will look at _Shavuos_ and the remaining holidays of the year from a Noahide perspective.

The Noahide Covenant & Man

To understand the Noahic significance of Sinai, we must place it within the context of God's historical relationship with man. When God created man, He did so with a number of hopes and expectations. However, God also gave man free will. By giving man free will, God also gave man the ability to disappoint Him as well as to please Him. As a result the God/man relationship is never a static one; is it constantly in flux as man provokes and God responds, or God provokes and man responds. The history of humankind, since the beginning of creation, is a chronicle of this dynamic and evolving relationship.

- **Year 1 / - C3760** – God creates Man. The Noahide laws, either all or in part, are communicated to Adam and Eve. This constitutes the first covenant with man.

- **Year 1536/-2225** – By this time man had completely forgotten, or willfully ignored, the original covenant. The world is completely corrupted and man follows his desires with no thought as to God's will. In this year, Noah began construction of the Ark.[1]

- **1657/-2104** – Noah and his family had remained in the Ark for a full solar year (the equivalent of one lunar year and 11 days).[2] Noah, his family, and all that was with him exited the Ark on the 27th or 28th of Cheshvan. Sometime during the waning days of Cheshvan and the first days of Kislev, Noah and his sons named the constellations in the sky.[3] Noah also gave offerings from the clean animals. At this time, God was appeased and resolved to never again destroy the world on account of man. God designated the rainbow as a sign of this covenant. God also commanded (or, according to some, only modified) the last of the Seven Universal Laws – the commandment against eating meat from the limb of a living animal.[4] Noah and his descendants were also granted all living things as food.

- **1996/-1765** – Within only a few hundred years the world had fallen back into idolatry and, with the exception of a very few individuals, the Noahide laws had been forgotten. In this year the peoples of the world were dispersed and their languages mixed as a result of the Tower of Babel.[5] According to many, it was at this time that Abraham recognized God's complete unity.[6] God also recognized the uniqueness of Abraham.

---

[1] See *Zohar, Bereshis 58b*; Rashi to Gen. 5:29.

[2] *Midrash Rabbah, Bereshis* 33:7.

[3] *Mishnah Torah, Yesodei HaTorah* 3:7.

[4] According to Maimonides, *Hilchos Melachim 9*:1, the first six Noahide laws were given to Adam and the remaining one given to Noah after the flood. *Tosafos*, however, holds that all seven were given to Adam and only modified in the times of Noah.

[5] See *Midrash, Yalkut Divrei HaYamim* I 1073.

[6] *Midrash Rabbah Bereshis* 64:4 and *Seder HaDoros*. Although Abraham rejected idolatry earlier in his life, it appears that it was not until age 40 or 48 that he came to a fully developed, monotheistic recognition of God. See Maimonides, *Hil. Avodah Zarah* 1:3 with *Hagahos Maimonios* and *Kesef Mishnah*.

- **2018/-1743** – God's relationship with Abraham ascended as the world fell deeper and deeper into idolatry and immorality. Therefore, God chose to make a new covenant with Abraham alone. In this year, the *Bris Bein HaBsarim* (Covenant of the Parts) is made with Abraham.[7]

- **2048/-1714** – The covenant of circumcision is made with Abraham.

- **2084/-1677** – Abraham and Isaac, his 36 or 37 year old son[8], were tried by the *Akeida* – the binding of Isaac. Their special relationship is further established with God.

- **2185/-1576** – Jacob dreams of the ladder. At this time, God continues his covenant with Jacob.

- **2238/-1523** – Jacob and his family descend into Egypt. Egypt is a furnace of idolatry, magic, necromancy, and everything antithetical to the faith of Abraham, Isaac, and Jacob. Nevertheless, in this, the capital city of spiritual impurity, despite 210 years of slavery and oppression,[9] the descendants of Jacob (known now as the Children of Israel) maintained their monotheism and allegiance to God.

- **2448/-1313** – God redeems the children of Israel from Egypt. He leads them to Sinai, where He establishes an eternal covenant with the entire people and reveals the Torah. Although Israel was God's primary concern at Sinai, it was not God's only concern. By the time of Sinai, the rest of the world had entirely abandoned the Noahide laws. With Israel's triumph of faith, God took new hope in the future of his creation. As He commanded Israel in the Torah, He also seized the opportunity to reaffirm the Noahide laws and command them anew to the world.

---

[7] See *Mechilta Shemos* 12:40; *Tosafos Berachos 7b* & *Shabbos* 10b; *Maharsha* to *Megilla* 9a; *Seder HaDoros*.

[8] This is based on the accepted chronology found in the *Midrash* and *Seder HaDoros*.

[9] Abraham is told that his ancestors will go into exile for 400 years; however this count began with Isaac and not with the actual descent into Egypt. The actual time of Israel in Egypt was only 210 years. See *Mechilta, Shemos* 12:40-41; *Seder HaDoros*.

From Sinai onwards, God's expectation for humanity was to observe the Noahide laws not because of their having been commanded to Adam or Noah, but because of their having been affirmed by Moses at Sinai. From this time onwards, the Noahide laws would be bound up with and subject to the interpretation and study of the Torah as revealed and entrusted to the Jewish people at Sinai.

Although the Seven Noahide Laws were commanded to the world in the times of Noah and Adam (as part of God's evolving relationship with man), their final form was established at Sinai. For Noahides today, Sinai is the origin, purpose, and motivation for keeping the Noahide laws.

This is the reason for Maimonides's words in the Mishnah Torah:[10]

> *All who accept the Seven Mitzvos and are careful to observe them are called* MiChasidei Umos HaOlam *(of the Pious Peoples of the World) and they have a share in the World to Come. This is provided that one accepts and observes them because they were commanded to him by the Holy One, in his Torah, and reaffirmed by Moses. However, one who observes them based on intellectual reason alone is neither called a* Ger Toshav *nor* MiChasidei Umos HaOlam *(of the Pious Peoples of the World). He is, rather, "of the wise ones" of the gentiles.[11]*

Shavuos, the anniversary of the giving of the Torah is the time to connect with the obligation of observing the Noahide laws, accept them anew, and celebrate the fact that God affirmed them anew at Sinai.

Judgment for the Fruits of the Trees

Our Mishnah, which we have seen many times, states:

> *At four junctures, the world is judged: on Passover for grain,* **on Shavuos for fruits**, *on Rosh Hashanah all pass before him like sheep of the flock, as it is written, "He*

---

[10] **Hilchos Melachim** 10:11.

[11] The text of this last phrase differs in the *editio princeps* (Rome, 1480) and almost all subsequent printed editions. These versions read : ... *one who observes them based on intellectual reason alone is neither called a* Ger Toshav *nor* MiChasidei Umos HaOlam *(of the Pious Peoples of the World),* **and is not** *"of the wise ones" of the gentiles.* This is almost certainly the error of a careless copyist (the mistake being in the transcription of a single letter). Many of the earliest manuscript versions read ... *He is, rather, "of the wise ones" of the gentiles.* Later scholars also cite this version of the text as correct. See Teshuvos Maharam Alashkar *117*, Rav Yosef ben Shem Tov's Kevod Elokim *29a*, and, more recently, Igeros Reiyah *I:89*. Recent critical editions of Maimonides have corrected this text to read ... *He is rather "of the wise ones" of the gentiles.* See Rabbi Shabtai Fraenkel's edition of the *Mishneh Torah*. See also the editions prepared by Rabbi Yosef Qafih and Yeshivat Or Vishua.

form their hearts as one, he understands all of their deeds." (Psalms 33). On Sukkot, the world is judged for water.

On *Shavuos*, the world is judged upon fruits. As such, it is an appropriate time to pray for the produce of trees.

Observances for *Shavuos*

Shavuot will next fall on May 24, 2015. Like all the holidays, it actually begins at nightfall on the preceding evening.

Decorating the Synagogue

There is a custom to decorate the Synagogue with greenery and flowers in commemoration of the revelation at Sinai, a mountain "full of greenery." The *Bnei Yissaschar* further connects this custom to the Midrash, which states the following:

> *To what can this [the revelation at Sinai] be compared? A king had a garden that had become overgrown with thorns. The king brought in gardeners to cut down the entire garden. Just then, the king saw a single rose blooming. He said: "For the sake of this rose, let the entire garden be saved!" Likewise, God declares: "In the Merit of the Torah, the entire world shall be saved!"*

In giving the Torah to Sinai, God took renewed hope in the world. This is confirmed by the fact that the Noahide laws were re-commanded to the World at Sinai. It is, therefore, appropriate for Noahides to decorate their places of worship or homes for the holiday in accordance with this Midrash and the other reasons that we have stated.

Renewed Acceptance of the Noahide Laws

Since this is the anniversary of God's affirmation of the Noahide laws to the world, this is an appropriate time to both individually and communally accept and affirm the Noahide laws. This acceptance does not require a Beis Din or witnesses, but may be done individually or personally. There is no set text for this acceptance; indeed Maimonides says that this is a matter entirely dependent upon the heart. However, should one wish to make a public declaration of his faith, we suggest the following text:

> *I accept upon myself the Seven Commandments of the Children of Noah, including the general and specific prohibitions of idolatry, murder, theft, sexual immorality, blasphemy, eating of flesh torn from a living animal, and the general and specific commandments to establish a system of justice, as commanded to Noah, Adam, and their descendants, by the mouth of The Holy One, creator of the universe, as reaffirmed and transmitted by His servant Moses at the giving of the Torah at Sinai.*

Prayers

Prayers should express the desire that the entire world acknowledge the revelation at Sinai and come to accept the Noahide laws.

Prayers should also include petitions for favorable judgment upon the produce of trees.

A Vigil of Torah Study

There is a Jewish custom to remain awake for the entire night of Shavuos, studying Torah in anticipation of the arrival of daybreak. There are a number of reasons for this custom, many of which connect it directly to events relevant to Israel. The *Magen Avraham*, for example, explains:

> The Zohar says that the early pious ones would stay awake all night on Shavuos and learn Torah. Nowadays, our custom is for most learned people to do so. Perhaps the reason is based on the fact that the Israelites slept all night long and God had to wake them when He wanted to give them the Torah, as it says in the Midrash, and therefore we must repair this.[12]

The Midrash records that Israel overslept on the Morning of receiving the Torah. For this reason, proposes the Mogen Avrohom, the Jews remain awake all night on *Shavuos*.

However, the Zohar records other reasons for this custom:

> R. Shimon used to sit and learn Torah at night when the bride joined with her spouse. It is taught: The members of the bride's entourage are obligated to stay with her throughout the night before her wedding with her spouse to rejoice with her in those perfections (tikkunim) by which she is made perfect. [They should] learn Torah, Prophets and Writings, homilies on the verses and the secrets of wisdom, for these are her perfections and adornments. She enters with her bridesmaids and stands above those who study, for she is readied by them and rejoices in them all the night. On the morrow, she enters the canopy with them and they are her entourage. When she enters the canopy, the Holy One, blessed be He, asks about them, blesses them, crowns them with the bride's adornments. Blessed is their destiny.[13]

This passage describes the giving of the Torah as a "wedding" of The Holy One to His Presence, the *shekhina*. Kabbalistically, this refers to the rectification and restoration of God's kingship in the world. This spiritual wedding is accompanied by the bridesmaids, the Jewish people, who learn Torah all night as an adornment of the bride. The Zohar offers further descriptions of this custom:

---

[12] *Mogen Avraham OC 494.*

[13] *Zohar* I:8a

8

> *Therefore, the pious in ancient times did not sleep that night but were studying the Torah, saying, "Let us come and receive this holy inheritance for us and our children in both worlds." That night, the Congregation of Yisrael is an adornment over them, and she comes to unite with the King.*
> *Both decorate the heads of those who merit this. R. Shimon said the following when the friends gathered with him that night: Let us come and prepare the jewels of the bride… so that tomorrow she will be bejeweled… and properly ready for the King.[14]*

It appears that the custom of staying awake all night is unique to the closeness of Israel and God. Nevertheless, it is appropriate to increase Torah study on this day and to prepare spiritually for the morning of Shavuos. It is, therefore, appropriate to gather and study the Noahide laws and Midrashim pertaining to the Noahide laws and the giving of the Torah until late at night. The morning prayers should be held early as well.

Tisha B'Av – the 9th of Av

Tishav B'Av, the 9th day of the month of Av, is the darkest day on the Hebrew calendar. On this date, innumerable tragedies befell the Jewish people throughout their history. Most importantly, both of the holy temples were destroyed on this day, albeit 500 years apart.

However, this day was fixed as a time of mourning long before, while Israel still wandered in the wilderness:

> *The Lord spoke to Moses saying, "Send out for yourself men who will scout the Land of Canaan, which I am giving to the children of Israel. You shall send one man each for his father's tribe; each one shall be a chieftain in their midst." So Moses sent them from the desert of Paran by the word of the Lord. All of them were men of distinction; they were the heads of the children of Israel…*

> *They returned from scouting the Land at the end of forty days… They brought them back a report, as well as to the entire congregation, and they showed them the fruit of the land… They spread an [evil] report about the land which they had scouted, telling the children of Israel, "The land we passed through to explore is a land that consumes its inhabitants, and all the people we saw in it are men of stature… **The entire community raised their voices and shouted, and the people wept on that night.**[15]*

---

[14] *Parashat Emor* 88a.

[15] Numbers, chapters 13 & 14.

The Midrash explains that God, upon hearing the people weep, said: "Since you have cried on this night for no reason, I will give you a reason!"

Because of the *lashon hora*, evil speech, which was perpetrated on this day against the land of Israel, the 9th of Av became designated as a day of sadness for all future generations.

Jewish Observance of *Tisha B'Av*

Tisha B'Av, the 9th day of Av, is a day of mourning for the Jewish people - not only for the Temple, but for all the tragedies of their history. Although a Holocaust memorial day has been recently established, it is not acknowledged by most observant Jews. Rather, they remember the Holocaust along with all other tragedies on *Tisha B'Av*. This is because *Tisha B'Av* is the root, the source, of all of these tragedies.

On this day, Jews fast from sundown until after sundown. Additionally, they gather in the synagogue and recite laments while seated upon the floor. There are a number of other observances expressing mourning that are kept as well. For example, Jews do not greet each other on this day. Additionally, they do not wear leather shoes or bathe. For Noahides, who do not share in the tragic history of the Jewish people, they cannot relate to much of the meaning of this day. However, Noahides do have a share in the most fundamental concern of the day – mourning the destruction of the Holy Temple.

Tisha B'Av & Noahides – Mourning the Temples

Though the service and responsibility of the Temple was given to the Jewish people, the Temple was of benefit to the entire world (as we have discussed much in our previous lessons). In fact, the sages tell us:

> *If the nations of the world had only known how much they needed the Temple, they would have surrounded it with armed fortresses to protect it!*[16]

On *Tisha B'Av*, Noahides, should they wish to fast in mourning for the temple, may certainly do so. However, it is suggested that this only be a half-fast, from sunset until noon of the following day. Additionally, it is appropriate to compose and recite

---

[16] *Bamidbar Rabbah 1:3.*

laments upon the destruction of the temples. These should be appropriate to the Noahide relation to the temples.

Point of Action:
Noahide *Kinnos*

The Jewish laments for *Tisha B'Av*, called <u>*Kinnos*</u>, are mostly relevant only to Jewish history and Jewish experience. It is appropriate for Noahides to compose their own *kinnos*, laments, for the day. These should be recited both at night and morning prayers.

Tisha B'Av is an opportunity to recognize the importance of the Temple, and to express to God the desire to right the wrongs of the world.

A service for the Noahide commemoration of *Tisha B'Av* is being drafted as part of this course.

Tisha B'Av will next fall on Sunday, July 26, 2015. As will all holidays, it actually begins on the preceding evening at nightfall.

Summary of the Lesson

1. While Jews celebrate Shavuos as the giving of the Torah, Noahides celebrate it as the day upon which the Noahide laws were renewed and a day of judgment for the fruit of trees.

2. The place of worship or the home should be decorated with greenery.

3. It is a time for reaffirmation and acceptance of the Noahide laws.

4. Torah study should be increased on this day.

5. On Tisha B'Av it is appropriate for Noahides to mourn the loss of the Temple and to meditate upon its meaning for the Nations of the world.

6. If Noahides wish to fast on Tisha B'Av, it should only be until midday on the day of Tisha B'Av.

7. It is appropriate for Noahides to recite laments for the destruction of the two Temples. This is a point of action for Noahides – to compose laments appropriate to their relationship with the temple.

The Noahide Laws - Lesson Thirty Five

164 Village Path, Lakewood NJ 08701 732.370.3344
164 Rabbi Akiva, Bnei Brak, 03.616.6340

Table of Contents:

1. Introduction

2. When Was the Mitzvah Given?

3. *Tzaar Baalei Chaim* – Animal Cruelty

4. The Commandment to Noah

5. *Ever Min HaChai vs.* the Verses

6. To Which Animals Does it Apply?

7. What is Called *Basar* – Flesh*?*

8. Summary

Introduction to Ever Min HaChai

Introduction

We now begin our study of the dietary laws applicable to Noahides. The most important prohibition in this arena is *ever min ha-chai*, that of a limb taken from a living animal. Though it may, at first, seem like a narrow prohibition, it actually involves a number of details.

When Was *Ever Min HaChai* Given?

As we should recall from a very early lesson, the Talmud derives all Seven laws from Genesis 2:16:

> *And the L-rd, God, commanded the man, saying: "Of every tree of the garden you may surely eat."*

Ever Min HaChai, besides being derived from this verse, was also commanded directly to Noah after the flood. There are two opinions as to the reason for this repetition. Both of these interpretations are tied to another Talmudic debate as to whether or not Adam was permitted to eat meat:[1]

---

[1] See Sanhedrin 57a, 59b.

- **Rashi**[2] & **Tosafos**[3] – Both hold that, as the Talmud states, all seven laws were given to Adam at the time of creation. This would include *ever min ha-chai*. Of course, *ever min ha-chai* would only be relevant if Adam was permitted to eat meat at this time. According to Rashi and Tosafos, Adam was permitted to eat meat; however, he was not allowed to kill animals for food. Adam was only allowed to eat animals that had died on their own. It was not until after the flood that Man received permission to kill animals for food.

- **Maimonides**[4] – Maimonides understands the Talmud's derivation of the Noahide laws from Genesis an *Asmachta*, a supporting allusion to the existence of the laws prior to the time of Noah. It is not a hard-and-fast source for their derivation. Based upon a much simpler reading of the Torah text, Maimonides proposes that man was not given permission to eat meat at all until after the flood. Therefore, Adam could not have been commanded regarding *ever min ha-chai*. It was only after the flood, when man was permitted from eating meat, that God gave the commandment against *ever min ha-chai*.

Both **Tosafos, Rashi** and **Maimonides**, however, agree to the following points:

- At creation, Adam was given the right to use animals for any useful tasks as the Torah teaches:[5]

  And God blessed them; and God said unto them: 'Be fruitful, and multiply, and replenish the earth, and subdue it; and have dominion over the fish of the sea, and over the fowl of the air, and over every living thing that creeps upon the earth.'

- This permission, however, did not extend to killing animals for food.[6]

---

[2] To Sanhedrin 57a.

[3] To Sanhedrin 56b.

[4] *Mishneh Torah, Hilchos Melachim* 9:1.

[5] Gen. 1:28.

[6] Sanhedrin 59a.

Considering these two points, of the utility of animals for human need vs. the prohibition of killing them for food, the question naturally arises: Was Adam allowed to cause pain or suffering to animals?

Tzaar Baalei Chaim – Animal Cruelty

The prohibition against animal cruelty, *tzaar baalei chaim*, applies to Noahides.[7] The exact details of this prohibition will be examined in greater detail in a future lesson. For the purposes of this lesson, though, we at least need to know that it applies and will be relevant to our study of the laws of *ever min ha-chai*.

The Commandment to Noah

In the times of Noah, all agree that man was given permission to now to kill animals for the sake of food:

The fear of you and the dread of you shall be upon every beast of the earth and every bird of the sky, upon everything that moves on the earth and upon all fish of the sea; into your hand they are given. Every moving thing that has life shall be yours for food; I have given them unto you like the green herbage.

The commandment of *ever min ha-chai* was either given here for the first time, or reaffirmed in light of this permission to kill animals for food:

But flesh with its soul, its blood, you shall not eat.[8]

The Talmud in Tractate Sanhedrin 59a explains that this verse is the prohibition of *ever min ha-chai*.

Ever Min HaChai vs. the Verses

The term *ever min ha-chai* is a Talmudic paraphrase of the source verse for the prohibition. It is a much more convenient and, indeed, specific way of referring to the law. However, it contains a subtle weakness.

---

[7] See *Sefer Toldos Noach* I: 26:11; *Sefer Sheva Mitzvos HaShem* IV: 1 *Haarah* 3. See also *Sefer Chassidim 666.*

[8] Gen. 9:4.

Ever min ha-chai is often translated as "a limb torn from a living animal." This is a terrible translation! The verse in the Torah states simply:

But Flesh with its soul, its blood, you shall not eat.[9]

The Talmud rephrases this prohibition as *ever min ha-chai*, which literally means "a limb/part from the living." Let's break it down:

- *Ever*, "a limb/part" – The verse states "flesh," a broad term we will have to winnow down. Although the Hebrew word for "flesh" is sometimes used specifically for "meat," in this context it means almost any edible part taken from an animal. The Talmud rephrases it with the term *ever* to capture the broader meaning of the word for "flesh." The intent of the prohibition is to prohibit any edible, solid parts separated from an animal while it lives.

- *Min*, "from" – The verse does not say anything about material being "taken" or "torn" from a living animal. Therefore, the method by which the material is separated from the animal is irrelevant. A limb remains prohibited even if it falls from an animal on its own. We should note that, according to this point and the previous one, one might incorrectly assume that even milk and eggs should be prohibited. We will therefore discuss milk and eggs in the next lesson.

- *HaChai*, "the living" – This last term is very broad. In fact, it is too broad, because the actual verse contains a qualification that limits the types of "the living" creatures to which this this applies:

*But **flesh with its soul, its blood**, you shall not eat.*[10]

Note that this verse draws a distinction between the flesh and the blood of the animal. This distinction actually has an important place in Torah law.

For example, for Jews consuming horse blood violates their injunction against consuming blood (the punishment for which is *Kares*, spiritual excision). Eating the meat of a horse, however, is prohibited to Jews for a

---

[9] Gen. 9:4.

[10] Gen. 9:4.

separate reason: the prohibition against eating the meat of non-kosher species (the punishment for which is lashes).

Our verse states the qualification *...flesh with its soul, its blood...* to teach us that the prohibition of *ever min ha-chai* only applies to animals for which the Torah makes legal distinctions between their *flesh* and their *blood*.[11]

There are many animals for which the Torah makes no distinction between their flesh and their blood. For these animals, the entire animal and all of its parts and pieces are included under one prohibition against eating. Since the Torah makes no distinctions for these animals, then *ever min ha-chai* does not apply to these animals.

To Which Animals Does it Apply?

Ever min ha-chai does not apply to *sheratzim*, a class of eight animals mentioned by the Torah in Lev. 11:29-30. This is because there is no distinction between their blood and flesh in Torah law. All of the commentaries agree that the common mouse and, most likely, the monitor lizard are among these eight creatures; however, there is disagreement as to the identity of the remaining 6. In practice, one should not eat any *ever min ha-chai* from any animal in which the application of *ever min ha-chai* is doubtful or a matter of dispute.

The following are the *sheratzim* with various opinions as to their identity:

- **Choled** – The Talmud describes this as a predatory, burrowing animal that tunnels underneath houses.[12]
  - Weasel/ermine/martin, mole, or mole-rat - According to the *Arukh*
  - Rat – *Targum Onkelos, Tosafos Yomtov*
  - Field Mouse – *Targum Yonasan*

- **Akhbar** – Most agree that this is the common mouse. Some include the rat under this term.

- **Tzav** – The Talmud[13] implies that it is similar to a salamander or snake.

---

[11] Sanhedrin 59a – b.

[12] See Shabbos 107a.

- o Toad – This is the opinion of Rashi to Lev. 11:29 and Niddah 56a. The Mishnah,[14] and indeed many of the *Rishonim*, seem to compare it to a frog.
- o Tortise – *Meam Loez, Tiferes Israel.*[15]

- **Anakah**
  - o Hedgehog or beaver – Radak.
  - o Gecko – Rabbeinu Saadia Gaon

- **Ko'ach**
  - o Lizard – According to *Radak.* From the descriptions of the various commentaries, it is most likely the monitor lizard.[16]

- **Leta'ah**
  - o Another species of lizard or great gecko.

- **Chomet**
  - o Snail – Rashi.
  - o Many other commentaries identify this as a skink.

- **Tinshemes**
  - o Mole – Rashi to Chullin 63a.
  - o A Burrowing lizard of some sort.

Further exempted from the prohibition of *ever min ha-chai* are all creatures that live entirely in the sea, insects, arachnids, and snakes, frogs, and lizards. It is therefore permitted consume limbs from dolphins, crabs, lobster, etc. before the animal has actually expired. However, it is preferable done in a manner that minimizes the suffering of the animal (because of the prohibition of *tzaar baalei chaim* – cruelty to animals). There are some further important clarifications to make:

---

[13] Chullin 127a.

[14] Tohoros 5:1. See Mishnah and Rishonim there.

[15] To Tohoros ibid.

[16] See Rav Saadia Gaon, in particular.

- **Rodents** – because of the uncertainty in identifying all of the *sheratzim*, and the doubt is on a biblically prohibited matter, one must treat all rodents as if *ever min ha-chai* applies to them. The exception, however, is the common mouse. It is certain that the mouse is a *sheretz* and that *ever min ha-chai* does not apply to it.

- **Seals, otters, walruses, etc.** – these mammals all live in the water as well as on land. Are they to be treated as sea creatures, and exempted from *ever min ha-chai*, or as land mammals and included in *ever min ha-chai*?

  - **Maimonides**[17] - Classifies sea lions as sea creatures, which implies that they are exempted from *ever min ha-chai*.

  - **Chullin 127a** – If a mammal can travel on land of its own power, then it is considered a land animal in *halakhah*.

  - **Mishnah, Keilim 17:13** – The carcass of a sea lion is subjected to certain types of ritual impurity that do not apply to sea animals. Therefore, the sea lion must be a land animal.

  - ***Tzafnas Paneach*** on Maimonides – Based on many of the cited rebuttals, *Tzafnas Paneach* rejects Maimonides as the law.

  - **In practice,** seals, otters, walruses, and similar creatures are considered land animals and subject to *ever min ha-chai*.

What Is Called *Basar* - Flesh?

The source verse prohibits *Basar* – flesh – from a living animal. This means that one is only liable for punishment for having eaten *Basar* from a living animal. However, this is a broad term which applies in various ways. Additionally, any prohibition against eating something only applies if that item is considered fit for consumption. The criteria for this determination are complex and require the expertise of a *posek*.

The following is a basic guide to what is and is not permitted. Again, note that we are dealing with what is called *basar* for the sake of liability. Eating any solid body parts

---

[17] *Hilchos Maachalos Assuros 2:12.*

from a species of living animal to which this prohibition applies is prohibited even if one does not incur punishment for doing so:

- **Bones** – Because bones are not considered fit for human consumption, they are not called *Basar*.[18] One should not eat them, however.[19] However, bone marrow is considered *Basar* – flesh.[20]

- **Tendons & Sinews** – Although not considered *Basar*, their consumption is prohibited. However, one is not liable to punishment for eating them.[21]

- **Hooves, horns, feathers** – These parts, even their soft inner parts, are not called *Basar*, and therefore *ever min ha-chai* does not apply.[22] Again, however, they should not be consumed.[23]

- **Flesh of Birds** – Although the prohibition applies to birds just as it does to land mammals, one is not liable to punishment for consuming bird flesh.[24]

- **Hides & Skins** – Some types of hides and skins are called *basar* and some are not. Any questions of *ever min ha-chai* that may arise regarding hides or skins should be presented to a *posek* who is an expert in the Noahide laws.[25]

- **Placenta** – A placenta expelled naturally by an animal may be eaten and is not included at all in the prohibition of *ever min ha-chai*. However, if it is removed from the animal before it gives birth, then it is prohibited as *ever min ha-chai*.[26]

---

[18] *Hilchos Maachalos Assuros 4:18.* This is true even if the bones are ground or powdered. Even soft chewable bones are exempted. See *Hilchos Avos HaTumah 3* and *Hilchos Korban Pesach 10.*

[19] Rama, YD 62.

[20] *Tosefta, Pesachim* 6:8.

[21] See *Hilchos Korban Pesach 10:8* and the commentary of the *Raavad* there.

[22] *Hilchos Maachalos HaAssuros 4:18* & *9:7*. See also *Avos HaTumah 1, 3:9*.

[23] See n. 19, above.

[24] *Hilchos Melachim 9:10* and *Kesef Mishnah* there.

[25] Maimonides, *Hilchos Maachalos Assuros* 4:18, states that hides and skins are not considered fit for consumption and that ever min ha-chai does not apply to them. This is even in a case when they are fully cooked and made appetizing (see Rashi to Chullin 77b). However, this is only the law for certain hides. "Soft" hides are considered Basar and are subject to ever min ha-chai. See Rashi to Chullin 122a and *Maachalos Assuros* 4:20-21.

- **Blood** – Blood is not included in the prohibition of *ever min ha-chai*. As we mentioned above, the Hebrew word *basar* – flesh – is broad and includes almost all solid parts of the animal. However, the source verse makes a clear distinction between blood and flesh:

*But **flesh with its soul, its blood**, you shall not eat.*

Maimonides[27] and *Kesef Mishnah*,[28] based on Sanhedrin 59a, explain that this prohibits *Basar* taken from an animal while it is living, but not blood taken from an animal while it is living. Blood may be consumed by Noahides even if it is taken from an animal while it is living.

Summary of the Lesson

1. *Ever min ha-chai* was either given to Adam or to Noah. This depends on whether or not Adam was permitted to eat meat from animals that died on their own.

2. Noahides are enjoined against cruelty to animals. The details of this will be discussed in a future lesson.

3. The prohibition applies to any *basar* – flesh – that came from an animal while it was living. It does not matter how this flesh was removed from the animal.

4. The prohibition applies to animals for which the Torah makes a legal distinction between their blood and their flesh. This means that aquatic animals, bugs, and reptiles and amphibians are not included in this prohibition.

---

[26] This distinction may be derived from *Maachalos Assuros* 5:13 and the comments of the *Raavad* there.

[27] *Maimonides Hilchos Melachim* 9:10.

[28] Ibid.

5. Only that which is defined as edible and is called *basar* is prohibited as *ever min ha-chai*. Nevertheless, one should refrain from eating anything solid that is separated from a living species of animal to which this prohibition applies. Though one may mistakenly think that this prohibition includes eggs and milk, we shall explain their details in a future lesson.

The Noahide Laws - Lesson Thirty Six

YESHIVA PIRCHEI SHOSHANIM
ישיבת פרחי שושנים

**Written by Rabbi Avraham Chaim
Bloomenstiel**
© **Yeshiva Pirchei Shoshanim 2014**

164 Village Path, Lakewood NJ 08701 732.370.3344
164 Rabbi Akiva, Bnei Brak, 03.616.6340

Table of Contents:

1. Introduction

2. Amount for Liability

3. The Life of the Animal

4. Strict Liability

5. Removing the Prohibition

6. Kosher vs. Non-Kosher Slaughter

7. Possible Leniencies

8. Practical Advice

9. Eating Out

10. Eggs and Milk

11. Summary

Ever Min HaChai II

Lesson

Introduction

Last week we saw the basis of *ever min ha-chai* and the scope of its application. This week we are going to look at more of the fundamentals of this prohibition and some challenges presented by the contemporary food industry.

Amount to Trigger the Prohibition

There is no minimum amount that a Noahide must consume to incur liability for *ever min ha-chai*.[1] Even the smallest amount of *ever min ha-chai* is enough to incur punishment. However, swallowing an entire living creature is not prohibited. After all, the prohibition only applies to meat which is "from" a living creature.[2]

The Life of the Animal

But flesh with its soul, its blood, you shall not eat.[3]

---

[1] Maimonides, Hilchos Melachim 9:10.

[2] This issue is debated in Chullin 102b. *Tosafos* rules like Rabbi Yehudah, that eating an entire living creature is not forbidden. Although Rashi disagrees, Maimonides upholds *Tosafos*. See *Hilchos Maachalos Assuros* 4:3.

[3] Gen. 9:4.

Rashi and *Targum Yonasan* make an important observation on this verse: that it applies to eating flesh while the animal's soul is "in/with its blood." As the sages understand this, the prohibition of *ever min ha-chai*, to trigger punitive liability, only applies while the animal from which the flesh was taken is still living. Once the animal dies, eating the flesh that was taken from it does not incur liability. However, the sages state that meat removed from an animal while it was living remains prohibited for everyone for all time - even after the animal has died:

> *Flesh that becomes detached from it [while it is dying] is considered like flesh detached from a living creature and is prohibited to a Noahide even after the animal has expired.*[4]

This point is very important and we will revisit it shortly.

Strict Liability

One only incurs strict liability, meaning capital punishment, if one transgresses *ever min ha-chai* by eating:

- Meat,

- From a land mammal,

- Removed from the animal while it is living,

- Eaten while the animal is still living, and

- Eaten in the normal manner.

All other possible "eatings" do not incur the death penalty, but are nonetheless forbidden. Therefore, though one is not punished for eating the flesh taken from a bird while it is still living, it is still forbidden to do so.[5]

---

[4] *Chullin 121b.* Although this is the law, the Talmud's exact reasoning behind the statement is a little unclear. According to many, it is a Rabbinic decree. Of course, this interpretation raises the debate as to if, how, and to-what-degree rabbinic decrees apply to Noahides. Others, however, take a much stricter approach. Nevertheless, all agree that the meat remains prohibited for all time even after the animal has died.

[5] See *Hilchos Melachim 9:10* with the *Kesef HaMishnah.*

Removing the Prohibition

There is a big difference between Jewish law and Noahide law as to when the prohibition of *ever min ha-chai* ceases to apply to an animal. For Jews, the process of *shechita*, Jewish ritual slaughter, removes the prohibition of *ever min ha-chai*. Once the majority of the trachea and esophagus of an animal has been severed according to Torah law, the prohibition of *ever min ha-chai* ceases to apply. At that point, a Jew may remove a limb or meat from the animal even if the animal is still in its death throes. That flesh would be permitted for a Jew to eat.[6] However, for a Noahide, the prohibition of *ever min ha-chai* does not depart from the animal until its heart has ceased beating.[7] This fact creates a contradiction between Jewish and Noahide law:

- If an animal is slaughtered properly, in accordance with the laws of Jewish ritual slaughter, it is considered "dead" for all intents and purposes even it is still moving about. A Jew may then sever and consume meat from that animal even before its heart and breath have ceased.

- However, the meat severed from that animal remains forbidden for Noahide consumption as *ever min ha-chai*. This is because Noahides do not rely upon ritual slaughter to remove the prohibition of ever min ha-chai, rather, they rely upon the death of the animal.

If you have been paying close attention, you will note a subtle problem: this situation appears to contradict our general rule from the Talmud that Noahide law cannot be more prohibitive in scope that Torah law.

The Talmud[8] and many *poskim* (most notably the *Shakh*[9]) explain that when a Jew slaughters meat for Jewish consumption, this slaughter completely removes the prohibition of ever *min ha-chai* in its totality - even for a non-Jew! This unique rule is subject to the following conditions, though:

---

[6] This is only in respect to *ever min ha-chai*. Practically, the animal remains prohibited for eating until it actually dies. See *Yoreh Deah 27*.

[7] See *Shulchan Aruch HaRav OC 329:3*. At that point we assume that all motion and breath have stopped. If the animal has ceased moving and breathing, and has bled copiously, then we may assume that the heart has stopped.

[8] Chullin 121b.

[9] To *Yoreh Deah 27*.

- It must be the slaughter of a kosher species,

- It must be slaughtered by a qualified *shochet* (slaughterer) according to all of the details of kosher *shechita,*

- It must be slaughtered for Jewish consumption,

- Once the animal has been slaughtered properly, meat may be removed from it even before it has stopped moving. However, one should wait until the animal has died before actually eating the meat.

Once these conditions are met, the meat of the animal is permitted for all, Jews and Non-Jews alike. Needless to say, kosher slaughter today is carried out according to all of these requirements. Therefore, non-Jews may consume kosher meat without any concern for *ever min ha-chai.*

But what about non-kosher meat production? Does non-kosher industrial slaughter present any problems for Noahides today?

Kosher vs. Non-Kosher Slaughter

The standard procedure in most non-kosher slaughter houses is to stun the animals (usually by electric shock) immediately prior to actually killing them. Although stunning may stop the animal's breath temporarily, it does not render the animal "dead enough" for the purposes of our removing the prohibition of a limb torn from a living animal.[10]

As for the actual methods of slaughter employed by most slaughterhouses, most of them do not bring about the immediate death of the animal (meaning complete cessation of cardiac and neuromuscular activity). Should the animal be conveyed to processing prior to the cessation of cardiac activity, a problem would arise as to the *kashrus* of the meat for Noahides.[11] This is because the animal would, effectively, be carved up before it has actually died and the meat rendered *ever min ha-chai.*

---

[10] See *Chasam Sofer YD* 339; *Shu"t Igros Moshe YD* II:146.

[11] These methods do, however, mortally wound the animal. In such cases, the meat is forbidden, yet one does not incur capital liability for having eaten it. See Radvaz to *Hilchos Melachim* 9:13 and *Sefer Sheva Mitzvos HaShem IV:3:2, haarah 71.*

According to Dr. Temple Grandin, one of the world's leading experts on industrial slaughter, the interval between slaughter and processing is so long that it is very rare for an animal's heart to continue beating until the time of processing. However, this generalization is not true of smaller slaughterhouses and specialty slaughterhouses (i.e. those that produce exotic meats). Although the stunning and slaughter of animals is strictly regulated by USDA policy, regulations pertaining to the time between slaughter and processing are uncommon at both state and federal levels and do not apply equally to all sectors of the meat industry.

Although the chances of getting *ever min ha-chai* at the grocery store are low, the only way to ensure beyond any doubt that your average grocery store meat is acceptable for Noahides is to know with certainty how the animal was slaughtered, and the policies of the slaughterhouse as to determining the death of the animal.

Considering that any amount of *ever min ha-chai* is prohibited for consumption, it is not unreasonable to be wary of commercially produced meat. By eating meat which has been slaughtered according to the laws of *shechita* (Jewish ritual slaughter) and relying upon the ruling mentioned above, any suspicion is removed.

Possible Leniencies

However, there are many possible leniencies for Noahides with regard to buying regular, grocery store meat. Unfortunately, these leniencies depend on whether or not certain mechanics of Torah law carry over into Noahide law. For example:

- **Safek** – Cases of doubt. The resolution of doubts as to whether or not an item is prohibited is governed by many principles and canons. Although these rules could create leniencies for Noahides with regard to non-kosher slaughtered meat, it is uncertain as to whether or not these rules apply in the Noahide legal system.[12]

---

[12] This question of *safek issur* by Noahides is discussed at great length by the *poskim*. Unfortunately, there is no consensus on the issue. The problem depends on a number of unresolved questions. First – are Noahides obligated in Rabbinic laws? Second – is the concept of *safek d'oraisa lechumra* ("biblical doubts are resolved stringently") itself sourced in the Torah (like Rasbha, *Chiddushim* to *Kiddushin* 73a) or in rabbinic legislation (like Maimonides in *Avos HaTumah 9:12*). If it is a matter of Torah law, then Noahides must avoid even doubtful transgressions of the Noahide laws. However, if it is rabbinic, then everything depends on whether or not Noahides are bound by rabbinic laws. This is an extremely complicated question. See *Toldos Noach* I:18:45 for an extensive survey of the literature. Incidentally, it is possible to prove from the *mitzvah* of *dinim* (establishing courts) that Noahides are obligated in Rabbinic law. For the purpose of this course, we take the

- ***Rov*** – Nullification by majority. If a prohibited item is mixed with a majority of permitted items to the point that we cannot distinguish between the two, then the prohibited item is considered "nullified" in the majority. It unclear if this principle applies to the Noahide laws.[13] If it does, then all mass produced meat may be considered "in a mixture" and, thus, the minority of meat coming from living animals is nullified in the majority of acceptable meat.

Though the application of these leniencies is doubtful, so too is the very presence of *ever min ha-chai* on the regular, commercial grocery market. Although each factor (*rov* or *safek*) by itself is not enough to permit the consumption of over-the-counter grocery store meat, taken together, most contemporary authorities agree that they may be relied upon to permit the consumption of regular grocery store meat.

Practical Conclusions

Despite the uncertainties as to the aforementioned leniencies, there are strong reasons to permit the Noahide consumption of regular, grocery store meat. As we said, though, there are reasons to dispute on this permissive approach.

Therefore, there is a stringent option for those who wish to adopt it. As we mentioned above, the act of Jewish ritual slaughter removes any doubt of "a limb taken from a living animal." Although regular non-kosher meat is permitted, should a Noahide wish, he may elect to consume only meat that was slaughtered according to Jewish ritual law. By doing so, all questions of *ever min ha-chai*, a limb from a living animal, are removed. According to many, this approach is proper and strongly supported by the aforementioned authorities on Torah law. However, one who does not wish to adopt this stringent approach has what to rely upon.

So, there are two approaches to dealing practically with the question of flesh from a living animal:

1) Regular, grocery store meat is 100% acceptable for Noahides. Even though there are uncertainties as to whether or not the concepts of

---

approach that Noahides are only obligated in the Rabbinic laws that apply to those *mitzvos* in which Jews and Noahides have equal obligation and that have logical application to both.

[13] As with cases of doubt, the rule of majority also depends on how we understand many of the underlying mechanics.

"nullification by majority" and "doubt" apply to Noahides, there are also uncertainties as to whether or not meat from living creatures is even present in the marketplace. Noahides may rely upon these two uncertain factors in combination to permit regular grocery store meat.

2) Because there are some who would question this leniency, a Noahide may voluntarily, and <u>as a stringency only</u>, elect to only eat meat that was slaughtered according to Jewish ritual practice.

<u>This second approach *does not* advocate or imply that Noahides are in any way obligated or expected to keep Kosher – the Jewish dietary laws.</u> The *only* reason for electing to consume kosher-slaughtered meat is that, by doing so, one can be guarded from any suspicion of *ever min ha-chai*, flesh taken from a living animal, according to most authorities. Observing this elective stringency does not constitute *chiddushei dat*, creating a new religion. The reason it is not *chiddushei dat* is that one observes this stringency only in order to avoid eating *ever min ha-chai*, flesh from a living animal. **<u>One does not observe this stringency to "keep kosher" or in any way imitate Jewish practice</u>**; after all, a Noahide has no share or obligation in such laws.

Keep in mind that, while this stringency is strongly supported and proper according to many, it is not necessary and purely voluntary. Practicing it has nothing to do with "keeping kosher" because the only reason for a non-Jew to eat meat slaughtered according to Jewish ritual law is because this is one of many possible ways of avoiding the prohibition of *ever min ha-chai*.

Eating Out

If a Noahide chooses to only eat kosher slaughtered meat, he will encounter problems when it comes to eating out. Non-kosher restaurants will have used their utensils and equipment for non-Kosher grocery store meat. Is it permitted for Noahides who have taken this voluntary stringency upon themselves to eat in such restaurants? Does a Noahide who has taken this voluntary stringency upon himself have to be concerned for the flavor of possibly *ever min ha-chai* meat that has been absorbed into the vessels?

The issue of absorptions in utensils is a major part of the Jewish dietary laws. The *poskim* disagree as to how or if it affects the Noahide laws.

- **_Chasam Sofer_**[14] - Pots and utensils that have been certainly used for *ever min ha-chai* may never be used by non-Jews.[15]

- **_Darchei Teshuvah_**[16] - The *Darchei Teshuvah* and many other *poskim* hold that there is no prohibition on Noahides using utensils that were previously and even certainly used with *ever min ha-chai*.

A Noahide who is careful to eat only meat slaughtered according to Jewish ritual practice may rely upon the *Darchei Teshuvah* and other *poskim* who permit utensils that had been used with *ever min ha-chai*. This is due to a solid *heter* (permissive ruling) from the *Darchei Teshuvah* combined with a number of other potential leniencies.

Of course, this only means that although Noahides who have accepted such a stringency may eat out at restaurants that serve regular, non-kosher meat, they may not eat any food containing actual meat at the restaurant. Again – this is only applicable to those who have elected such a stringency. However, this stringent approach is not at all required or expected.

Eggs & Milk

Technically, eggs and milk should be included in the prohibition of *ever min ha-chai*.[17] After all, they are material separated from the animal while it was living. This possibility does not create a problem for Jews, because the Torah explicitly permitted eggs and milk to them:

- "…A land flowing with milk and honey…"[18] The Talmud says that by praising Israel with milk, this verse is permitting milk, exempting it from the prohibition of *ever min ha-chai*.[19]

---

[14] *Shu"t YD 19*, at the very end.

[15] According to the *Chasam Sofer*, the *heter* of *linas laila* and *taam pagum* does not apply to Noahides.

[16] 62:5.

[17] Talmud *Bechoros* 6b to 7a and *Tosafos Chullin* 64a, d.h. *Sheim rikmah*.

[18] This phrase appears in many verses in the Torah.

[19] See Talmud ibid.; Rosh 1:5.

- The Torah states: "If you chance upon a birds nest on your way, in a tree or on the ground, with young ones or eggs, and the mother is sitting upon the young, or the eggs, you shall not take the mother with the young[20]" This is understood as releasing eggs from the prohibition of *ever min ha-chai*.[21]

These verses, however, were only given to Israel – they do nothing for Noahides. Are Noahides are still prohibited from eating eggs and milk?[22]

Although the *Chasam Sofer*[23] suspects that certain eggs are, in fact, prohibited to Noahides, almost all other *poskim* disagree. Virtually all *poskim* permit milk for Noahides.[24]

The reasons that milk and eggs are permitted for Noahides will be discussed in the live class.

Summary of the Lesson

1. Although the requirements to trigger punishment for transgressing *ever min ha-chai* are very narrow, the scope of the prohibition is very broad.

2. Technically, one is not liable for punishment for *ever min ha-chai* unless the animal from which the meat is taken is still living at the time the meat is consumed.

3. There a number of potential issues with commercially produced non-Kosher meat. These issues do not exist with meat slaughtered according to Torah law. For many reasons it is advisable, according to many, for

---

[20] Deut. 22:6.

[21] See *Bechoros* ibid.; *Chullin 140a; Tos. Chullin 64a.*

[22] Practically speaking, nearly all *poskim* agree that milk and eggs are permitted for Noahide consumption. However, their reasons for permitting them are greatly varied and not at all simple.

[23] YD 19.

[24] Rabbi Shlomo Kluger in his *HaElef Lecha Shlomo YD* 322 brings a proof from Avraham, who served dairy to his guests.

Noahides to eat meat that is slaughtered by a Jew according to the laws of Jewish ritual slaughter law. Nevertheless, regular grocery store meat is permitted for Noahide consumption.

4. Noahides who observe the stringency of eating only meat slaughtered according to kosher practice may eat out at any restaurants as long as they do not eat the meat served there.

5. Milk and eggs are permitted for Noahide consumption even though there are theoretical reasons to consider them *ever min ha-chai*.

The Noahide Laws - Lesson Thirty-Seven

164 Village Path, Lakewood NJ 08701 732.370.3344
164 Rabbi Akiva, Bnei Brak, 03.616.6340

Table of Contents:

1. Introduction

2. Two Reasons

3. Modern Applications

4. *Stam Yayin* - Wine

5. *Chalav Akum & Gevinas Akum* – Milk & Cheese

6. *Pas Akum* – Baked Goods

7. *Bishul Akum* – Non-Jewish Cooking

8. *Sheichar Akum* – Social Drinking

9. Transporting Kosher Foods

10. Summary

Kashrus III

Introduction

In this last lesson on dietary laws we are not going to discuss Noahide prohibitions, rather, we are going to discuss a number of prohibitions that apply only to Jews. The reason we are discussing these laws here is because they affect the relationship between Jews and non-Jews. Food is a major factor in building social bonds and relationships. All too often, the Jewish dietary laws present challenges for Jews and non-Jews. The issue, however, is not merely one of ingredients. As we shall see, Torah law places limits on Jewish and non-Jewish social interactions, using food to define the boundaries of these relationships. It is important to understand the basis and reasons for these restrictions so that either group does not offend one another or come to misunderstanding.

Two Reasons

These prohibitions are motivated by two concerns. Some are due to the possibility that non-kosher material may be present. Others were established for the express purpose of limiting social contact between Jews and non-Jews. This group of prohibitions was established out of concern for intermarriage between Jews and non-Jews; an extremely severe prohibition with equally severe consequences.

Modern Applications

Even though many of the reasons behind these prohibitions are not relevant anymore in our times, they nevertheless continue to apply. This is because of a principal in Torah law called *davar she-biminyan*.[1] This principle teaches that decrees established by ancient courts cannot be overturned by later courts unless they are equal in number and eminence to the original court.

Stam Yayin - Wine

Wine that is owned or made by a non-Jew is prohibited for Jewish consumption. This is so even if all of the ingredients and utensils used in the process of manufacture are kosher. Included as well is any wine or grape product has been touched, moved, or poured by a non-Jew. The rabbis made this decree out of concern for the intent of the non-Jew at the time of handling the wine. If the non-Jew had any thoughts or intent for idolatry at that time, the wine would become biblically prohibited to Jews like an idolatrous offering. Today, this law applies in a slightly different way than it did in ancient times. This is because the idolatry of today differs from ancient idolatry. Nevertheless, many elements of this law are still an application to all grape-juice, wine, and grape derivatives. Because of *davar she-biminyan* (discussed above), this law applies even to wine touched by Noahides and even those in the process of conversion to Judaism.

Though this prohibition applies to all grape juice, wine, and grape byproducts, it does not apply to wine or grape juice that has been boiled or cooked. This is because the ancient forms of idolatry that motivated the original prohibition did not consider cooked wine fit for religious use.

Therefore if you are at a gathering of Jews at which wine is served, make sure that the wine is *Mevushal*, cooked, before handling it. If it is not cooked, then it should not be handled or moved. Similarly, if bringing wine to a dinner, one should only give wine that is *Mevushal*. This is usually indicated on the label, near the *hekhsher* (symbol of kosher approval):

---

[1] *Beitza 5a.*

Lastly, kosher wine that remains corked and sealed cannot be rendered prohibited until it is opened.

Chalav Akum & Gevinas Akum - Milk & Cheese

Milk and cheese produced by non-Jews, even if all of their ingredients are kosher, is nevertheless prohibited for Jews. This is because non-kosher material may have been mixed into the milk or the cheese. In order for non-Jewish milk or cheese to be kosher, a Jew must have been present while the cheese was made or the milk was milked.

These laws have very little impact on regular Jewish and non-Jewish interactions. Nevertheless it is good to be aware of them.

Pas Akum - Baked Goods

Bread and other baked goods baked by a non-Jew for personal use are prohibited for Jewish consumption. This is even in a case when all of the ingredients and the oven involved were kosher. This decree was made purely to limit the social interaction between Jews and non-Jews. Resultantly, bread that was baked for commercial purposes, meaning for sale and not for consumption, may be eaten by a Jew and is not subject to this prohibition. Therefore, a Jew cannot eat cookies baked for him by a non-Jewish friend, but a Jew can purchase the exact same item at the grocery store.

Bishul Akum - Non-Jewish Cooking

Many other items cooked by a non-Jews are prohibited for Jewish consumption. This is, again, even if all of the ingredients and utensils used are kosher. However, this law only applies to foods which have a certain degree of "significance." The details of what is considered "significant" for the purposes of this law are complicated and not always a matter of consensus. Generally speaking, very basic staple foods, such as coffee and tea, and certain basic snacks (like potato chips, according to some) prepared by a non-Jew may be eaten by a Jew.

However, almost all other items are considered prohibited for Jewish consumption. As well, the utensils used by the non-Jew in preparation of these foods are also prohibited for use by a Jew. If food is later cooked by a Jew in these utensils, that food would also prohibited for Jewish consumption.

Practically speaking, this prohibition makes it impossible for a Jew to ever permissibly eat food of any kind that has been prepared in the home of a non-Jew. This was, after all, the fundamental intent of this law.

The only exception to this law is if a Jew has minimal participation in the cooking. Ashkenazim and Sephardim have different understandings as to what is called "minimal participation."

Sheichar Akum - Social Drinking

This prohibition is one that, unfortunately, is not even known by many Jews.

Jews are not permitted to drink socially with non-Jews. Specifically, this refers to gatherings in which the purpose is to socialize and drink. It does not apply to situations in which the gathering has a primary purpose and alcohol just happens to be served. For example, if a Jew attends a conference with his coworkers, and beers happened to be served, or there is an open bar, a Jew may be allowed to have a drink. However, this is only if the occasion is infrequent. If the event or circumstances occur regularly, the Jew would not be allowed to drink. For example if a company gets together once a week to discuss business matters, and alcohol is always served at these meetings, a Jew would be prohibited from partaking in the beverages.

Similarly Jew cannot accept an invitation from a non-Jew to "come over and have a beer." However, if the Jew is in your home for some other reason (business, helping you move, etc.) then he may accept the offer of a drink. This law also forbids Jews from attending bars - an environment designed for social drinking. According to some authorities, this law does not only apply to alcohol, but to all "social beverages." Therefore, getting a cup of coffee at Starbucks would also be

---

[2] YD 114. The application of this law depends greatly on existing social conventions and other details that change with time. As a result, the *Shulchan Aruch* is not the final word on this prohibition. Deciding questions pertaining to this law require familiarity with the decisions of later *poskim*. This section is based mostly on *Sefer Bein Yisrael LeNochrim* 11:8:23; *Chelkas Binyamin* 114:12; *Shut Halachos Ketanos* 9; *Bais Yehudah* 21; *Sheeilas Yaavetz* II:142; *Chochmat Adam* 66:14; *Shut Rivevot Ephraim* 6:79; *Shut Chai HaLevi* 4:53:6-7.

prohibited. Most authorities, though, point out that coffee houses are not places of socializing like bars. After all, people who congregate in coffeehouses usually do so in small groups or individually and rarely speak to strangers. Therefore, a Jew may get coffee in a coffee house, but is prohibited from getting alcohol in a bar. Nevertheless a Jew may not regularly go out regularly with non-Jews or a non-Jewish group and get coffee for the purpose of socializing.

Transporting Kosher Foods

Food transported or entrusted to a non-Jew, even if being sent from one Jew to another, is subject to a number of rules.

- All food requires at least one seal. The type of seal will be discussed in the live class.

- Wine, meat, chicken and fish require two seals.

In certain situations, the absence of such seals will render the food non-kosher when it arrives at its final destination. This *Halacha* contains a number of nuanced details. A *posek* should be asked in any situation in which a question arises.

Summary of the Lesson

1. Certain prohibitions were decreed on non-Jewish foods either out of concern for kashrus or to limit social interactions.

2. These prohibitions apply today regardless of whether or not the underlying reasons for the prohibitions still exist.

3. Wines owned, made, touched, poured, or handled by non-Jews become prohibited for Jewish consumption. The exceptions are wines that remain fully sealed and corked or that are *Mevushal*.

4. There are similar laws pertaining to milk and cheese, however these don't have much practical effect on Jewish/Non-Jewish interactions today.

5. Anything baked by a non-Jew for consumption is prohibited to Jews. This is true even if all the ingredients are kosher. However, if baked goods are made for commercial sale, then they are permitted.

6. Any food cooked by a non-Jew is prohibited for Jewish consumption. This is even if the food is cooked in a Jew's home using the Jew's utensils. The pots and pans used for this cooking are even rendered non-kosher. The only way to permit a Jew to eat non-Jewish cooking is if a Jew participates, even minimally, in the cooking. There are differing opinions between Ashkenazi and Sephardi authorities as to what is called "minimal participation."

7. Social drinking between Jews and non-Jews is prohibited. A Jew cannot get a drink at a non-Jewish bar. Although this prohibition would technically include coffee houses as well, most authorities do not extend the prohibition that far.

8. A non-Jew cannot transport or hold onto food on behalf of a Jew unless the food is wrapped and sealed. Different foods require different types of seals.

The Noahide Laws - Lesson Thirty-Eight

© Yeshiva Pirchei Shoshanim 2017

164 Village Path, Lakewood NJ 08701 732.370.3344
164 Rabbi Akiva, Bnei Brak, 03.616.6340

Table of Contents:

1. Introduction

2. Sexual Morality & Derivations of the Laws

3. Example: The Canaanites

4. Categories of Prohibited Relations

5. Source of the Basic Subdivisions

6. Prohibited by Early Decree

7. Permitted, yet not Practiced

8. Male & Female Liability

9. Precautionary Laws

10. Summary

Lifecycle I: Male & Female

Lesson
38

Introduction

The next several lessons will cover the Noahide lifecycle from birth to death. In this lesson we will start just before birth: with the details of dating and marriage. This lesson will cover acceptable marriage partners, details of interactions between the genders, and issues of modesty in these areas.

Sexual Morality & Derivations of the Laws

The Noahide laws prohibit acts of sexual immorality. As discussed in a very early lesson, the Talmud learns these laws, by way of implication, from Genesis 2:16. Like all the Noahide laws, though phrased in the negative, it also implies positive aspects. Laws that prohibit sexual immorality also imply the converse: the embracing of acts of sexual purity and endorsing sexual morality.

As we have further seen, the seven Noahide laws are "families" of laws instead of discrete prohibitions unto themselves. Indeed, "sexual immorality" is too broad a term to mean anything without subdivision and definition. These laws, however, are unique because the Torah itself appears to provide many examples of what is and is not acceptable behavior.

For example:

- The behavior of Pre-Flood Society:

    The land was corrupt before G-d… For all flesh had corrupted its way.

The Talmud states: A braisa of the academy R' Yishmael has taught: anywhere that the term "corruption" is used, it is only in reference to sexual matters or idolatry.[1]

- Sodom & Gemorah

- The abominations of Egypt: *You shall not commit the deeds of the Land of Egypt wherein you dwelt.*[2]

  Although this was commanded to Jews, the Torah and Midrashim describe Egypt's deeds as "abominations." Many commentaries discuss whether this implies that the deeds of Egypt are prohibited to Noahides as well.

- Behavior of the Canaanites:

  Likewise, the deeds of the land of Canaan, the where I shall bring you, you not do; neither shall you walk in their statutes[3]*; and,*

  There shall not be found among you one who asses his son or daughter through the fire, one who uses divinations, and illusionist, an auger, or a sorcerer… because of these abominations, Hashem your G-d is banishing them from before you.[4]

  The Talmud states: God would not punish these nations unless he had warned them against such acts.[5]

The implication of these examples is not always clear. Let's take a close look at the Canaanites.

---

[1] Sanhedrin 57a.

[2] Lev. 18:3

[3] Lev. Ibid.

[4] Deu. 18:10-12.

[5] Sanhedrin 56b.

Example: The Canaanites

The Torah, in Lev. 18:3, introduces the list of Jewish prohibited relationships with the following:

You shall not commit the deeds of the Land of Egypt wherein you dwelt. Likewise, the deeds of the land of Canaan, the where I shall bring you, you not do; neither shall you walk in their statutes.

The Torah then goes on to list all of the relationships prohibited to Jews in verses 6 to 24. The Torah concludes by stating that the Canaanites lost their land to Israel as punishment for transgressing the laws of sexual morality:

And the land was defiled, therefore I visited their iniquity upon it, and the land vomited out its inhabitants. Therefore, you shall keep My statutes and My ordinances, and shall not do any of these abominations; neither the native-born, nor the convert, for all these abominations have been committed by the men of the land who came before you, and the land is defiled...[6]

Does this Lev. 18:3, referring to the "deeds of Canaan," imply that the succeeding list of prohibited relationships (verses 6 to 24) equal the abominations committed by Canaan? If we say "yes," then all of the relationships mentioned in 6 to 24 are also prohibited to Noahides. However, if we say "no," then we cannot assume that all relationships in the list are prohibited to Noahides.

A proof may be adduced from the Talmud, Sanhedrin 56b. Deut. 18:10-12 lists a number of prohibited forms of sorcery and divination, stating that these were also reasons Canaan was driven from its land. The Talmud states: *God would not punish these nations unless He had warned them against such acts.*

However, things are not so simple. The Talmud[7] notes that there are relationships mentioned in the list that are, elsewhere, defined as permitted to Noahides. Therefore, the list in verses 6 to 24 cannot be defining the prohibited Canaanite practices. Furthermore, not all of the Tannaim agree to the idea that *God would not punish these nations unless He had warned them against such acts.* If so, then why then does the Torah appear to list these relations as the prohibited "abominations" of Canaan?

As we see from this example, the Torah's many references to what is or is not acceptable for Noahides, based on ancient practices, cannot be taken at face value.

---

[6] Lev 18:28.

[7] Sanhedrin 56b.

Categories of Prohibited Relations

There are a number of categories in this prohibition:

- **Relationships that are biblically forbidden** – We will see shortly how these are derived.

- **Relationships that are prohibited by decrees of ancient Noahides (i.e. Shem)** – the sages record a few relations that, although permitted by the Torah, were prohibited by ancient Noahides and their courts. Their ability to make such prohibitions, as we shall see, derives from the *mitzvah* of *dinim*, establishing rule of law. A few of these decrees continue to apply today, yet there are others that either do not apply today or whose application is uncertain.

- **Permitted, Yet Not Practiced** – As mentioned in the above discussion, the Torah refers to a number of relationships as "abominations" even though they are fundamentally permitted to Noahides. Is this term meant to imply that they are only abominations from the viewpoint of the Jewish *mitzvos*? Or, is it saying that they are abominations even when committed by non-Jews? The problem is the word "abomination," a term meaning socially, morally, or emotionally repulsive behavior. It is out-of-place in a discussion of law. Yet, if the permission/prohibition of an act is based on a social judgment or emotional reaction to an act, then the act must have been considered repulsive even before it was prohibited by law. Yet, we see that many of the acts called "abominations" in Lev 18:6-24 are not prohibited to Noahides. The conclusion, as we shall see, is that these acts are permitted, yet should not be practiced.

Source of the Basic Subdivisions

*Therefore, a man shall leave his father and mother
and cling to his wife and they shall become one flesh.*[8]

From this verse the Talmud derives five prohibitions for the descendants of Adam:

---

[8] Gen. 2:24.

- ***Therefore, a man shall <u>leave his father</u>...*** The Talmud explains that "leaving his father" means that one cannot have relations with that which is or was his father's, meaning his father's current or former wife. This applies for all time, even if one's father has died or has divorced the woman.[9] What makes the woman prohibited to the son (or the son to her) is that she and the father had formed a bond of marriage. This bond created the prohibition. The definition of this bond will be discussed below.

- ***...and <u>mother</u>...*** Using a similar reasoning as in the previous case, this prohibits incest between a man and his mother. The prohibition of relations between a man and his biological mother is prohibited even if the woman was never actually married to the man's father.[10]

- ***...and cling to <u>his</u> wife... <u>His</u>*** wife and not the wife of another man. This forbids adultery between a man and a woman who is another man's wife. This prohibition is based on the marital bond, which will be explained below. We should note that polygamy is permitted to Noahides as it is for Jews. However, Jewish courts universally banned the practice over 1000 years ago. For reasons that will be discussed in the class, this should not be practiced by Noahides either.

- ***...to his <u>wife</u>...*** This forbids male homosexual relationships. *Wife*, being of female gender, precludes a relationship between a male and a male. Lesbianism, although it cannot be derived from this verse, is nevertheless prohibited. The source for its prohibition is not agreed upon by all. Some view it as a subcategory or derivation from male homosexuality. Others prohibit it because it is one of the "abominations" practiced in Egypt, in combination with a number of other concerns. It may also be the subject of an earlier decree.

  The Talmud indicates that granting civil recognition to homosexual unions (equating them with marriage) is prohibited for Noahides.[11]

---

[9] *Hilchos Melachim 9:6.*

[10] *Hilchos Melachim ibid.*

[11] In <u>Chullin 92b</u>, Ulla laments that the Non-Jews of his time were sunk in the grossest forms of idolatry and immorality. However, he praised them for retaining three practices: 1) they did not write a marriage contract for homosexual unions, 2) they did not sell flesh in the marketplace (it is unclear to what this refers – see Rashi), and 3) despite all of their idolatry and immorality they still showed respect for the Torah.

- *...and they shall become **one flesh**.* This indicates the ability of a man and a woman to create *one flesh*, a child, through their union. This precludes relations between species that cannot produce offspring. Hence, all forms of bestiality are prohibited, whether one is male or female, or the active or passive partner.

There is a sixth biblical prohibition of incest between siblings. However, this prohibition does not have as clear a derivation as the others:

> *And Avimelech said to Abraham: 'What motivated you to do such a thing [to say "she is my sister"]?' And Abraham said: 'Because I thought: Surely the fear of God is not in this place, and they will slay me on account of my wife. And moreover she is indeed my sister, the daughter of my father, but not the daughter of my mother; and so she became my wife.*

From here, the authorities derive that a maternal half-sister, and all the more-so a full sister, is prohibited. The bond of marriage between any of the parents of these siblings is irrelevant here. Biological relation is enough to establish the prohibition.[12] Curiously, this only prohibits a sister with whom one is maternally related. Paternal half-sisters are permitted for marriage.[13] It appears that having the same mother is the benchmark for the biblical definition of siblings for the purpose of this prohibition. The exact reasons for this are a matter of interpretation.[14]

Prohibited by Early Decree

We know of a few prohibitions prohibited by early decree. However, it is clear that this category included many other relations not mentioned here. The "abominations" that are fundamentally permitted to Noahides may be relations that were voluntarily prohibited by the early Noahides. Therefore, although they are permitted, they are unacceptable. The following decrees, however, we know with certainty to be binding even today:

---

[12] *Issurei Biah 2:2-4.*

[13] Maimonides *Hilchos Melachim 9:5* and *Hilchos Issurei Biah 14:10.*

[14] The Jerusalem Talmud, *Yevamos 11*, however, derives the prohibition of sibling incest from Gen. 2:24, along with all of the other biblical prohibitions. However, even the Jerusalem Talmud debates as to whether or not it applies to all type of siblings.

- **Father and Daughter** – Another omission from this list is relations between a daughter and her father. Fundamentally, such relationships are not prohibited.[15] However, <u>Nachmanides</u>[16] and <u>Rashi</u>[17] write, that this practice was banned in the very early days of mankind as a repulsive practice.

- **Noahide & Idolater** - In the story of Judah and Tamar, we have to ask: by what authority was Judah able to decree death for Tamar? The Talmud in <u>Avodah Zarah 36b</u> records that, in ancient times, Shem and his court prohibited Noahide cohabitation and marriage with idolaters. The reason is that a family's religious commitment cannot be built on two faiths. Inevitably, one will be forced to assimilate or be subjugated to the other. Therefore, Noahides may not marry practicing idolaters. The commentaries explain that his decree stands until today.

  This is only discussing when a committed Noahide knowingly marries an idolater. Any other situation (i.e. one becomes a Noahide after having already married) is not included in this decree. Any practical questions as to how this applies must be presented to a competent *posek*. We will discuss this in much greater detail in the live class.

Permitted, yet Not Practiced

There are a number of other unions that, although fundamentally permitted, the Torah appears to condemn them as "abominations."[18] This is an extremely murky area. For reasons that will be discussed in the live class, caution is appropriate in all of the acts defined as "abominations" of Egypt and Canaan. Such acts include:

- One should not marry his mother's full or maternal half-sister. However, a paternal half-sister of his mother is completely permitted.[19]

---

[15] Sanhedrin 58b; Shulchan Aruch YD 29:3.

[16] Gen. 19:32.

[17] Gen. 20:1.

[18] See *Sifrei* and *Peirush HaMishnayos*, Sanhedrin 7. These are derived from many of the above mentioned verses pertaining to the Canaanites and Egyptians. Although these acts are fundamentally permitted, and one does not incur punishment for doing them, the Torah itself may dissuade them, calling them "abominations." See Maimonides Hilchos Issurei Biah 14:10.

[19] Nachmanides to Yevamos 98; Shulchan Aruch Yoreh Deah 269:3.

- Some hold that some paternal aunts are also called "abominations."[20] However, this conclusion is doubtful.[21] [Editor's Note: I do not see sufficient reason for stringency in this particular situation; it would be a *chumra yeseira* — an unsubstantiated stringency. The reasoning of the *Shach*, who bring this rule, is far more than just "doubtful." See footnote 21]

- Marrying a both woman and her daughter (his stepdaughter). Although it is fundamentally permitted,[22] it is also called an abomination.[23]

- Uncle, brother, or son's ex-wife.[24]

This is only a partial list and many other relationships may be included. There is ample proof[25] that the generations immediately after the flood took on additional, voluntary prohibitions in sexual matters. Although it is unclear as what all of these prohibitions are, they may have included these things labeled "abominations" in Egypt and Canaan that are, technically, permitted to Noahides. If this is the case, then all of these "abominations" would be called "prohibited by early decree."

Male & Female Liability

All of the above categories of prohibited relations apply equally from both the female and male sides. The Talmud learns this from the phrase "…**they** shall become one flesh." Therefore, a woman's maternal half-brother is prohibited to her just as a man's maternal half-sister is prohibited to him. A woman is prohibited to her son just as a man's mother is prohibited to him.

---

[20] *Shach to Yoreh Deah 269:4.*

[21] [Rabbi Bloomenstiel: This *Shach* contradicts the generally held view of the Rishonim. As we saw in very early lessons, an *Acharon* (i.e. the *Shach*) cannot contradict a consensus of *Rishonim*. This particular issue depends on a dispute between Rabbi Eliezer and Rabbi Akiva in Sanhedrin 58b. Though the Shach follows Rabbi Eliezer, this is against the majority of the Rishonim (Maimonides, Nachmanides, Smag, etc.) who conclude that the law is like Rabbi Akiva.]

[22] Nachmanides, *Rashba, Nemukei Yosef* and other Rishonim to Yevamos 98.

[23] *Mitzvos HaShem* p. 398. *This is among the relations termed "abominations" by the Sifra to Lev. 18:3.*

[24] Ibid. and Shulchan Aruch Yoreh Deah 269.

[25] *Bereshis Rabbah* 70:12 & 80:6.

Defining Marriage

The details of Noahide marriage will be dealt with at great length in a future lesson. We must at least define marriage here because many of the prohibitions we have discussed depend upon it. Marriage is a means by which a woman becomes prohibited to all other men except for her husband. The man, by way of marriage, accepts certain obligations of support and protection for his wife.[26] By pursuing the ideal of Marriage, both parties are fulfilling the divine expectation of *yishuv haaretz*, settling and civilizing the world (which we will also discuss in a future lesson). For Noahides marriage involves, minimally, two components:

1) **A mutual agreement to accept the status of husband and wife and the prohibitions and expectations that come with that status.** Once this agreement has been made, the man and woman are considered betrothed. At this point, all the prohibited relations discussed above take effect. However, one is not yet liable for punishment for transgressing them.

2) **Consensual intercourse.** Once this has taken place, the man and women are liable for both transgression and punishment for all of these prohibitions.

Once a couple has fulfilled these two requirements, they are considered husband and wife in Torah law.

A man and woman who live together for an extended period of time may acquire the status of "betrothed," even if they have never agreed to do so. In certain situations, they may even be considered married.[27] As such, both would acquire the prohibitions and statuses implied therein. For this reason, it is not advisable for a man and woman to live together prior to marriage.

Precautionary Laws

In Jewish law there are a number of restrictions on interactions between the genders. For example, a man and woman who are prohibited to each other may not hug, hold hands, kiss, or engage in any other expression of physical intimacy (this does not apply to parents and their children or siblings – a parent may kiss or

---

[26] These obligations, however, are not explicit Torah obligations. According to many, they may fall out under the family of *dinim*, establishing rule of law, because society determines the moral and legal expectations of a man for his wife. For Jews however, these obligations are very strictly defined by the Torah.

[27] This issue impacts both Noahides and Jews. See *Hilchos Kiddushin 1*.

THE YESHIVA PIRCHEI SHOSHANIM SHULCHAN ARUCH PROJECT
THE NOAHIDE LAWS | NOAHIDE LIFECYCLE I | MALE & FEMALE | LESSON 38

hug his child). Similarly, such a couple may not be isolated together in an inaccessible or locked room.

Do these prohibitions apply to Noahides as well?

- **_Minchas Chinuch_**[28] – Yes. These prohibitions on contact and situations are not safeguards. Rather, they are intrinsically part of the biblical prohibitions. One does not transgress the biblical prohibition only by sexual congress, but by any pleasurable physical contact. This view is heavily disputed by other authorities and may only apply to Jews.

- **_Bereshis Rabbah_ 70:12 & 80:6** – Yes. The generation after the flood accepted extra precautions on issues of sexual morality. However, we cannot use the Midrash as a proof because it is not clear if these precautions were general precautions on physical contact and intimate situations. We only know for certain that these measures included precautions on specific relations between specific partners.

- **_Chavas Yair_**[29] **and _Chida_ as cited in the _Sdei Chemed_**[30] - No. A proof can be made by comparison of the laws pertaining to relations between Jews and non-Jews and the laws of relations between Noahides and Noahides. However, it is not clear that the situations mentioned are analogous. In the laws pertaining to relations between Jews and non-Jews, all of the restrictions involved fall on the Jew's side, not on the Non-Jew's. The fact that these prohibitions (from the Jew's side) are the dispositive ones is not proof that Noahides have no such prohibitions (we will clarify this in the live class).

- **_Mitzvos HaShem_**[31] – Yes. Noahides are forbidden to have contact or create situations that could lead to transgression. However, this purely is a logically compelled practice, and not an actual Torah obligation.

The _Mitzvos HaShem_'s point is the most compelling. It makes sense because there is a general principle that we can never trust ourselves when it comes to the sexual desire.[32]

---

[28] Mitzvah 188.

[29] 108.

[30] III: 38.

[31] P. 479.

[32] This is repeated many times in the Talmud and other Torah literature.

Since these precautions have a practical motivation, a Noahide may practice them even according to the Jewish laws. Many recent writers and teachers on Noahism have advocated that Noahides do so.

With tremendous deference and respect to these writers, it appears that their endorsement of this practice for Noahides may not be fully thought-out (this will be discussed more in the live class). For many reasons, Noahides must determine their own boundaries in these matters within a very broad set of guidelines.

For example, Noahides should use only Jewish law to determine what is permitted to them in these areas, and not what is forbidden in these areas. For example:

- A doctor seeing a female patient in an examination room – since this is permitted for Jews it is certainly permitted for Noahides.

- Socially acceptable forms of greeting (handshakes), since fundamentally permitted to Jews, are always permitted for Noahides.

As far as prohibitions are concerned, their determination is based on sensibility. Rabbi Bloomenstiel has suggested that any situation in which a wife would just have to "trust her husband," or a husband would have to "trust his wife" would be a situation that calls for precautions. The nature of these precautions is up to Noahides to determine. Such situations would include:

- **A man taking a business trip with a married female co-worker.**

- **A girl living in a college dorm.** Technically, premarital intimacy is permitted for Noahides. However, there are reasons to be strict that will be discussed in the live lesson.

- **A woman allowing another man into her home for a social visit if her husband is out of town. This is in a case when they would be alone.**

- **A man sleeping in or sharing a room with a man who is suspected of homosexual desires or activity**.

Socially acceptable forms of greeting (handshakes, etc.) are always permitted for Noahides.

Contact that implies intimacy should not be had between those who are prohibited to each other. The exceptions are normal expressions of love between immediate family members. This will be discussed in the live lesson.

Summary of the Lesson

1. Even though the Torah includes many apparent examples of sexual immorality pre-Sinai, these examples are not always clear prohibitions.

2. The fundamental prohibitions are learned from Gen 2:24 and from Abraham's words to Avimelech.

3. Many relations were prohibited by Noahides in ancient times. Only a few are known for certain to be in effect today. However, this may have included those things permitted for Noahides, yet called "abominations."

4. There are a number of relations that are fundamentally permitted, yet should not be practiced.

5. Liability for transgressing these prohibitions falls upon both the male and female transgression of these laws.

6. Marriage is the result of 1) agreeing to become man and wife, and 2) consensual sexual relations.

7. Logical precautions should be observed to avoid coming to transgress these laws.

The Noahide Laws - Lesson Thirty-Nine

164 Village Path, Lakewood NJ 08701 732.370.3344
164 Rabbi Akiva, Bnei Brak, 03.616.6340

Table of Contents:

1. Introduction

2. Source for Marriage

3. Implications of the Marital Concept

4. The Obligation of *Yishuv HaAretz*

5. Marriage

6. Beyond the Minimum

7. Sources & Suggested Elements for a Marriage Service

8. Common Law Marriage

9. Summary

Lifecycle II: Marriage & Pre-Marriage

Introduction

In the last lesson we saw the various prohibited relations and the need for reasonable precautions when it comes to interactions between the genders. In this lesson, we are going to discuss pre-marriage and marriage.

Source for Marriage

Therefore a man shall leave his father and his mother and cling to his wife, and they shall become one flesh.[1]

We have learned that this verse is the source of five of the six punishable prohibited relations. However, this verse also states that a man should "cling to a wife." This implies that marriage is the ideal relationship between men and women.

Yet, we must ask: Does marriage even apply to Noahides? This question hinges on a principle that we learned in an earlier lesson: **Anything stated before Sinai only applies to Noahides if it was repeated at Sinai.**[2] Therefore, if marriage was mentioned at Sinai, this repetition would be sufficient proof that the concept of marriage applies to all man. Sure enough, Deut. 22:13 states:

---

[1] Genesis 2:24.

[2] This is a fundamental principle of deriving the Noahide laws from Sanhedrin 59a.

380

When a man takes a wife…

In fact, the Talmud devotes an entire tractate, *Kiddushin*, to identifying and analyzing the numerous post-Sinaitic references to marriage. We see then that marriage applies to Noahides as well as to Jews.

Implications of the Marital Concept

Therefore a man shall leave his father and his mother and cling to his wife,
and they shall become one flesh.

Having established that the concept of marriage applies to Noahides, we have to then consider both its positive and negative implications.

The positive implication of marriage is that a committed, legally defined, consensual relationship is the ideal for Noahide men and women.

The negative implication of marriage is that noncommittal, undefined, or nonconsensual relationships are the opposite of that ideal. Nachmanides to Gen. 2:24 writes that the verse warns against promiscuity and licentiousness. However, the *poskim* do not derive or specify any prohibited acts of licentiousness (premarital sex, prostitution, etc.) The negative implications of our verse are too broad to imply specific prohibitions. Keeping this point in mind, let's examine another factor.

The Obligation of *Yishuv HaAretz*

The Lord, Creator of the Heavens, He is the God, the one Who formed the earth… He did not
*create it for emptiness, **he fashioned it to be inhabited…**[3]*

The phrase …*he fashioned it to be inhabited…* carries *halachic*, practical, weight.

---

[3] Isaiah 45:18.

Talmud Gittin 41a-b

The Talmud in Gittin 41a-b discusses the case of a Canaanite indentured servant who is granted partial release by his employers.[4] In this situation, his status is in serious doubt. Is he a Jew or a Non-Jew? The Talmud, Tosafos,[5] Rashi, and other commentaries explain that this "half-free" status is untenable. In such a state the person cannot marry a Jew or a non-Jew and, as the commentaries explain, cannot fulfill his obligation of *yishuv ha-aretz*, making the world settled and civilized. We see that *yishuv ha-aretz* is an obligation for Noahides.

Yishuv HaAretz, settling and civilizing the world, appears to be part of the commandment of *dinim*, establishing civil law. Along with the ideal of marriage and its negative implications against promiscuity, these concepts create a general obligation to avoid licentiousness and socially corrosive sexual behaviors.

However, the specifics of these obligations are not mentioned in any of the *halachic* codes. It may be that these general, conceptual prohibitions were the basis upon which the court of Shem and other early leaders decreed specific prohibitions for Noahide society.[6] This view may also explain the wording of I Kings 14:24, which states:

> *...and also prostitution was in the land, and they did all the abominations of the nations...*

The verse separates prostitution and the other "abominations" (prohibited relations), implying that they are problematic for different reasons. According to our understanding, prostitution had reached the point that it ran afoul of *yishuv haaretz* and the implications of the marital ideal. However, the "abominations," as we mentioned in the last lesson, may have been things that were decreed as prohibited by Shem and early Noahide courts. Therefore, they are "abominations," socially and morally reprehensible behaviors. However, prostitution is not called an "abomination," because it was connected to an actual prohibition.

---

[4] Once a Canaanite becomes a servant to a Jew, he is no longer a Jew or a Non-Jew. Instead, he attains a halfway-conversion of sorts: partially non-Jew and partially Jew. Upon gaining complete release from his servitude, the Canaanite is now a Jew in all respects. The situation under discussion is the status of a Non-Jew who is granted incomplete release. What then is his status?

[5] *Tosafos* to *Gittin* and also to *Bava Basra* 13a.

[6] As discussed in the previous lesson.

Prostitution and premarital relations, though not intrinsically prohibited, become problems when they impinge on the aforementioned obligations. Therefore, they are not punishable offenses. Noahides have an obligation, though, to regulate or discourage such behaviors as needed to preserve society.[7]

Marriage

Maimonides, based on the Talmud's discussion of pre-Sinaitic marriage,[8] writes in *Hilchos Ishus* 1:1 that prior to Sinai Noahides became married via a two-stage process.[9] This process is not meant to represent the ideal method of marriage, but only the absolute minimum requirements to affect marriage within the Noahide laws. Let's look closer at what these two factors entail:

1) **Agreement to become married:**

    a. The man and woman must be biblically permitted to each other. No bond of marriage exists between parties who may not marry each other on a biblical level.[10]

    b. No one can marry another against his or her will.[11]

    c. Additionally, one must be mature enough to understand the seriousness of the commitment and the prohibitions and the obligations that it entails. Therefore, there is a minimum age for marriage. This age is certainly no less than the age-of-obligation[12] within the Noahide laws, and may even be higher. If a man and women are not capable enough for marriage, then allowing them

---

[7] See *Even HaEzer* 177 and Rashi to Num. 22:5.

[8] Sanhedrin 57b – 58b.

[9] See Maimonides and Sanhedrin ibid; *Kiryas Sefer* and *Maggid Mishneh* on Maimonides ibid.; *Minchas Chinuch* 35:13 & 19; *Shut Rivash* 398. See also *Tosafos HaRid* to Bava Basra 16b, Rashi to Sotah 10a. There are far more sources and authorities than can be listed here.

[10] *Parshas Derakhim* and many others. See also *Shevus Yaakov* I:20 who clarifies that no status of marriage can exist between Jew and non-Jew either.

[11] Nachmanides *Milchamot* to Sanhedrin 8; *Nemukei Yosef* Sanhedrin 8; Ran to *Pesachim* 2; See also Rashi to Gen. 24:57.

[12] There is a dispute as to whether this is a fixed age or is dependent upon the individual's intelligence and understanding. This age will be the topic of a future lesson.

to marry is actually a detriment to society. Noahides should make these determinations for themselves.[13]

d. Both parties must understand and consent to the prohibitions and obligations that marriage creates. For example, the woman becomes prohibited to all other men. Similarly, the man must knowingly accept any obligations he may have to his wife.[14]

e. Once the couple has made this agreement, the woman is considered *meorasah*, "betrothed." At this point she is prohibited to all other men. However, she would not be liable for punishment if she should transgress.[15]

2) Consensual marital relations:

a. Having become betrothed, the marriage is consummated through consensual, normal[16] relations with the specific intent of creating the marital bond.[17]

b. Once the marital act is completed, the woman is considered a *be'ulas ba'as*, a fully married woman.[18]

Beyond the Minimum

There is no requirement for witnesses or ceremony for a Noahide marriage. However, we must keep in mind that that *halacha* – Torah law – provides a skeleton, an outline, in which to cultivate meaning, relevance, and importance. It is essential to make Noahide ceremonies meaningful, personal, and relevant to the spouses and their families.

---

[13] The Acharonim discuss the issues in this paragraph at great length. See *Shut Chasam Sofer YD* 317; *Minchas Chinuch 190*; Rashi to Nazir 29b; *Sdei Chemed Peas HaSadeh III*; *Hilchos Melachim* 10:2.

[14] A Noahide man has no biblical obligations to his wife. However, there are certain expectations that are compelled by the concept of marriage and *yishuv haaretz*. We will see these soon.

[15] See note 8 for sources.

[16] "Normal relations" refers to vaginal intercourse in the normal manner. See *Talmud Yerushalmi Kiddushin 1:1*.

[17] See Maimonides *Hilchos Ishus 1:1*; *Shut Rivash* 398; *Minchas Chinuch* 35:13 & 19.

[18] See note 8 for sources.

Additionally, since the process of marriage changes the status of the partners involved, it is appropriate to hold a service in which their new statuses are witnessed and announced to the world.

Sources and Suggested Elements for a Marriage Service

- **Wedding Canopy** – Getting married beneath a canopy is a requirement of Jewish law. Some _Rishonim_, however, imply that it is not a Jewish innovation. Indeed, they state that it was part of the marriage ceremony even in ancient pre-Sinaitic times. This is certainly not enough evidence to imply that one _should_ use a marriage canopy. However, it is enough to prove that it is acceptable for Noahides and doing so is not considered _chiddushei dat._ After all, the symbolism of the canopy applies equally to both Noahides and Jews (this will be discussed in the live class).

- **Wedding Rings** – the Talmud in Sanhedrin 58a writes that when a Noahide's marriage ends, the woman "uncovers her hair in the marketplace." In other words, she goes about bareheaded in public. Some have cited this passage as proof that married Noahide women should cover their hair.[19] However, it appears that the issue is not covering hair, but that the woman should have a public sign that she is married. Since this is the underlying reason, then covering the hair would not accomplish this purpose. After all, most people would not interpret it as a sign of marriage. However, a wedding ring certainly accomplishes this in America. Therefore, it is appropriate to give rings as part of the ceremony of marriage. Once the couple is married, they should be careful to wear their rings whenever in public.

- **Marriage Document** – Because accepting the obligations and prohibitions associated with marriage requires full knowledge and consent of the parties, these obligations and expectations must be specified and known to both the man and woman. The best way of guaranteeing this is for the parties to write vows and acknowledge them to each other. These vows should mention the prohibitions created by marriage and the obligations of marriage. Alternatively, and perhaps more effectively, would be to draft a list of the mutual agreements

---

[19] _Sefer Sheva Mitzvos HaShem VI:6:9._

of the husband and wife. The following is a suggested outline for such an agreement:

On the _____ day of the week, the _____ day of the month of _____ in the year _____, here in the city of _____, ___(groom)___ said to his bride, _____: "Please become my wife according to the laws of Noah as commanded to the world in ancient times and reaffirmed through the hand of Moses at Sinai. I pledge to _____, and I accept all of the expectations and obligations of a husband unto his wife, as well as any prohibitions created unto me by becoming your husband. Together we will build a home and, together, fulfill the divine vision of yishuv ha-aretz, settling and civilizing the world according to God's will."

On this day, _____ said unto her groom: "I will become your wife, according to the laws of Noah as commanded to the world in ancient times and reaffirmed through the hand of Moses at Sinai. I pledge to_____, and I accept all of the expectations and obligations of a wife unto her husband, as well as any prohibitions created unto me by becoming your wife. Together we will build a home and, together, fulfill the divine vision of yishuv ha-aretz, settling and civilizing the world according to God's will."

Before all of the undersigned, the bride and groom have together entered into the bond of betrothal with the intention of creating a complete bond of marriage.

_____   _____
Groom   *Bride*

_____
Witnesses

De Facto (Common Law) Marriage

We should note that an unrelated man and woman who live together without being married may acquire the de facto status of marriage or betrothal.[20] For this reason, it is not advisable that Noahide men and women share living spaces together prior to marriage.

---

[20] See *Hilchos Ishus 1:1* and commentaries. This is written about extensively in the *poskim* and commentaries.

Summary of the Lesson

1. Gen. 2:24 introduces the concept of marriage. The fact that it is iterated at Sinai indicates that it applies to Noahides as well.

2. Marriage implies not only what is appropriate, but what is inappropriate. However, it does not do so with enough specificity to imply particular prohibitions.

3. The Talmud states that *yishuv haaretz*, settling and civilizing the world, is an obligation of all mankind. For Noahides it implies certain prohibitions and responsibilities.

4. Minimally, marriage requires full agreement to accept the status of marriage and consummation via relations.

5. Although this is the minimum, it is important that the deeper, human and spiritual aspects of marriage be acknowledged and celebrated.

6. Noahides may use a wedding canopy.

7. One should possess a sign that she is married.

8. Since complete knowledge is required to accept the status of marriage, it is advisable that the bride and groom have some sort of a marriage document or vows that acknowledge their obligations and expectation.

The Noahide Laws - Lesson Forty

© Yeshiva Pirchei Shoshanim 2017

164 Village Path, Lakewood NJ 08701 732.370.3344
164 Rabbi Akiva, Bnei Brak, 03.616.6340

Table of Contents:

1. Introduction

2. Reproduction & *Yishuv HaAretz*

3. Conception & Contraception

4. *Coitus Interruptus*

5. The Marital Bond & Sexual Intimacy

6. Condoms

7. Surgical Sterilization

8. Pharmaceutical Contraceptives

9. Summary

Lifecycle III: Conception & Contraception

Introduction

In the last lesson we explored marriage, the beginning of the Noahide lifecycle. In this lesson we move onto the next stage: starting a family. This lesson will address questions of conception and contraception, touching on a number of other issues along the way.

Reproduction & *Yishuv HaAretz*

Adam and Noah were both commanded in "be fruitful and multiply." However, this commandment was not repeated at Sinai. As we learned in prior lessons: any *mitzvah* given before Sinai, yet not repeated at Sinai, applies only to Jews.[1] Therefore, *peru u'revu*, be fruitful and multiply, is not a Noahide *mitzvah*.

In the last lesson, we learned about the obligation of *yishuv haaretz*, settling and civilizing the world. This commandment includes the expectation of reproduction and building a family. What is the difference, though, between the commandment of *yishuv haaretz* and *peru u'revu*, "be fruitful and multiply? If they are the same, then why do we need them both?

---

[1] Sanhedrin 59a.

3

There are big differences between the two *mitzvos*:

- **Yishuv HaAretz** is a general obligation to reproduce, raise children, and through doing so build and perfect human society. This applies to both men and women.

- **Peru U'Revu,** "be fruitful and multiply" is a very specific commandment applying only to Jewish men. One fulfills this commandment by fathering at least 1 boy and 1 girl. Furthermore, it creates a number of de facto negative commandments. For example, contraception is technically prohibited until this *mitzvah* is fulfilled.[2]

Conception & Contraception

May contraception be used by Noahides? What if a man and woman want to wait to have children? What if pregnancy would pose medical risks to the woman? There is no Torah-based reason to prohibit contraception for Noahides. However, certain methods of contraception may pose problems. Let's examine them one-by-one:

Coitus Interruptus

At first glance, it appears *coitus interruptus* is absolutely prohibited. After all, the Talmud tells us this practice is one of the acts that brought the flood.[3] Furthermore, Er and Onein, the sons of Judah, were specifically punished for doing this.[4]

However, things are not as clear as they look. Before Sinai, Noahides were obligated in "be fruitful and multiply." After Sinai, they were not.[5] Therefore, we have to ask the question:

---

[2] There are a number of allowances for contraception depending on the circumstances of the couple. Jewish couples must consult a *posek* to determine when contraception may be used.

[3] Rashi to Niddah 13a; Sanhedrin 108b. Genesis 6:12 states: "All flesh has corrupted its way upon the earth," is understood by the Talmud as a reference to onanism.

[4] Gen. 38:9. See Yevamos 34b for the Talmud's discussion of their deaths.

[5] Sanhedrin 59a.

Were Er, Onain, and the generation of the flood punished for an independent transgression of spilling seed? Or, was it because they had spurned their obligation of "be fruitful and multiply?"

If they were punished for spilling seed, then it may apply even to Noahides today. However, if it was due to "be fruitful and multiply," then it is not relevant to Noahides today.

Another issue depending on this question is the permissibility of male masturbation. If the prohibition is only because of spurning "be fruitful and multiply," then male masturbation may be permitted to Noahides. However, if it is an independent prohibition of spilling seed, then male masturbation is specifically prohibited.

Tosafos to Sanhedrin 59b takes the latter approach: Er, Onan, and the generation of the flood were punished for spurning "be fruitful and multiply." Since this obligation does not apply to Noahides today, there is no reason why the acts of Er, Onan, etc. should be prohibited.

However, Nachmanides[6] holds that spilling seed is a prohibition independent of "be fruitful and multiply.[7]" All of the other major Rishonim (Rashba, Ran, Ritva and others) concur with him. This would mean two things:

1) *Coitus interruptus* is a prohibited form of contraception, and
2) Male masturbation is prohibited.

Accordingly, any form of contraception that wastes seed should be prohibited. This would preclude the use of condoms. The same reasoning would also prohibit sexual relations with a woman who is infertile. However, there is another factor to consider.

---

[6] In his novellae on the Talmud.

[7] There is some disagreement as to Nachmanides's underlying reasoning. See *Mateh Aharon* cited in *Sdei Chemed* VII and *Mishneh LaMelech* to *Melakhim* 10:7. They read Nachmanides as saying that this is a biblical prohibition. However, *Toras Chesed* to *Even HaEzer 43* argues that Nachmanides's understands this is a rabbinic prohibition. However, *Pnei Yehoshua* II EH 44 brings strong proofs that this prohibition is biblical. According to the *Pnei Yehoshua*, anytime the Torah says something is "wicked in God's eyes," it is communicating an absolute biblical prohibition upon all peoples.

The Marital Bond & Sexual Intimacy

Part of the marital bond, and even a prerequisite of it, is the sexual intimacy between a man and a woman.[8] Sexual intimacy is as much a special part of the marriage as emotional, spiritual, and intellectual intimacy. The sex act does exist merely for procreation, but is essential to establishing a bond between a man and a woman. Sex is not viewed in Torah religious thought as sinful, taboo, or purely utilitarian. In the right context it is meant to be indulged and enjoyed.

The *poskim*[9] have written extensively on this topic and their conclusions are universal: expelling seed during intercourse is part of the act of sexual intimacy between a man and woman. Therefore, even though a woman may be infertile, there is no issue for her husband from the side of "spilling seed." However, as we see from the example of Er and Onan, the semen must not be expelled outside of the woman's body.

Condoms

The problem with condoms is that the man's semen is collected within and then discarded. Obviously, this should violate the prohibition of "spilling seed." However, it is not so clear. Since expelling seed is permitted as part of marital intimacy, perhaps the use of a condom is permitted. After all, the seed is not expelled outside of the woman's body when a condom is used.

The *poskim* discuss and compare condoms to IUDs, which are permitted.[10] Both devices block semen from reaching the uterus, and all agree semen that later exits the woman's body poses no issue for the man. He is only liable for semen actually expelled outside the woman's body. The question comes down to whether or not the complete imposition of a condom between the man and woman makes it as if the semen is expelled outside the woman's body and therefore is not truly part of the marital act.

---

[8] Most *poskim* learn this from the implication of the phrase in Gen 2:24: "…shall cling to his wife…" the word for "clinging" in Hebrew connotes sexual as well as other forms of intimacy.

[9] The conclusion brought here is accepted as a fact in Torah law by all *poskim*. For specific details of the derivations and proofs, see Rabbeinu Asher cited in *Bais Yosef* to *Even HaEzer* 23. See also *Rama*, *Bach*, and *Bais Shmuel* cited there.

[10] See *Shut Achiezer* III:24; *Shut Maharshag* II:243; *Pri HaSadeh* III:53; *Igros Moshe* EH I:63.

Although the *Sefer Sheva Mitzvos HaShem* (*The Divine Code*) permits the use of condoms, the issue does not appear to be conclusively decided.[11]

Surgical Sterilization

The Tannaim[12] dispute whether or not sterilization is an independent biblical prohibition for Noahides. Rabbi Chidka and the School of Manasseh hold that it is a biblical prohibition from the verse:

…swarm on the earth, and multiply upon it…[13]

However, the other Tannaim view this verse as a statement of blessing, not a commandment.

The Rishonim and Acharonim are divided as to which Tannaic opinion is the *Halacha*, actual practice:

- There is an independent prohibition of sterilization – The Talmud rules that a Jew may not have a Noahide to castrate his (the Jew's) animal.[14] The reason, apparently, is that a Noahide is enjoined against castration.[15] The Jew, by asking the Noahide to carry out such an act, is "placing a stumbling block before the blind."

- There is no prohibition against sterilization – Most later *poskim* reject this line of reasoning, pointing out that a Jew is also prohibited from asking a Noahide to do anything that he himself, as a Jew, cannot do. Since Jews are biblically prohibited from sterilization, they may not ask a Noahide to

[11] Pirchei Shoshanim consulted a number of *poskim* on this question. Of the two American *poskim* consulted, one tentatively permitted condom use and the other held it was prohibited. Rav Bloomenstiel consulted *HaRav HaGaon* Chaim Kanievsky, *shlit"a*, one of the leading *poskim* in the world, who said: "Possibly, it is permitted. There is no liability [punishment] for doing so." The Rav was clear that this was not a *psak*, a conclusive statement. Similarly, *HaRav HaGaon* Shmuel HaLevi Wosner, *ztz"l* said that he has not yet seen any strong proofs to decisively permit or prohibit condom use for Noahides and that the issue still requires study.

[12] Sanhedrin 56a.

[13] Gen. 9:7.

[14] Bava Metzia 90b and numerous commentaries.

[15] See *Kiryas Sefer* on Issueri Bia 16:13. See also the discussion in the *Beis Yosef* on *Even HaEzer* 5.

do so. However, there is no implication that Noahides are also prohibited from castrating animals.[16]

Although the issue continues to be debated, it appears as if this discussion has passed into the realm of academic speculation. The large majority of *poskim* permits sterilization to Noahides and bring strong reasons for their rulings.[17]

While the *Halacha* is that there is no independent prohibition of sterilization for Noahides, *sterilization* poses another issue.

As we will learn in future lessons, a person is forbidden from causing any destruction or permanent damage to his body.[18] This includes many surgeries not deemed medically necessary.[19] Without a compelling medical reason, surgical sterilization should not be used as a method of contraception.

Tubal ligation however, does not appear to pose a problem.[20] Today, it is a relatively minor, reversible procedure causing no permanent damage to the body.

Pharmaceutical Contraceptives

Pharmaceutical contraceptives (such as "the pill") which do not result in any permanent physical damage are certainly permitted.[21] Similarly, a woman may use contraceptive film or foam.

---

[16] See Maimonides, *Issurei Biah* 16:13 with the *Maggid Mishnah*. See also the *Maggid Mishneh's* commentary to *Hilchos Sechirus* 13:3; Rosh, Rashi, and others to Bava Metzia 90a.

[17] It is difficult to find any contemporary *poskim* who rule there is a prohibition of sterilization for Noahides. The following is just a sampling of the more authoritative and extensive treatments of the subject: *Arukh HaShulchan, Even HaEzer* 5; *Shut Nishmas Chaim* 133; *Shut Zivchei Tzedek CM* 2; *Chelkas Yaakov Even HaEzer* 28; *Shut Ateres Paz* I, YD 14 & EH 7.

[18] The *Minchas Chinuch*, though he appears to hold that sterilization is an independent prohibition, adds that causing harm is another reason to prohibit.

[19] Cosmetic surgery, in many situations, is an exception to this rule. We will discuss it in a future lesson.

[20] *Igros Moshe, Even HaEzer* III:15.

[21] *Shulchan Aruch, Even HaEzer* 5:12.

Summary of the Lesson

1. Noahides are not obligated in *peru u'revu*, be fruitful and multiply. However, they are obligated in *yishuv haaretz*.

2. Contraception is permitted for Noahides. However, certain methods pose issues.

3. *Coitus interruptus* is prohibited to both Noahides and to Jews.

4. Sex is not purely utilitarian in Torah thought. It is part of forming the bond between husband and wife and is meant to be enjoyed.

5. Condoms are a permitted form of contraception for Noahides.

6. Surgical sterilization is prohibited if it renders one permanently sterile.

7. Pharmaceutical contraception is permitted.

THE YESHIVA PIRCHEI SHOSHANIM SHULCHAN ARUCH PROJECT

The Noahide Laws - Lesson Forty-One

164 Village Path, Lakewood NJ 08701 732.370.3344
164 Rabbi Akiva, Bnei Brak, 03.616.6340

Table of Contents:

1. Introduction

2. WARNING

3. Abortion in the Noahide Laws

4. At What Point is Abortion Prohibited

5. When the Mother is Endangered

6. Die or Transgress

7. *Rodef*: The Pursuer

8. Summary

Lifecycle IV: Abortion

Introduction

Abortion is an issue that evokes strong responses from everyone. Unfortunately, the possibility for nuanced and sensitive discussion of the important questions involved is marred by the existence of two dogmatic camps: "pro-life" and "pro-choice."

The Torah view of abortion does not fall clearly in either camp; both are contrary to the Torah view. From an ethical standpoint, the Torah views abortion negatively. The Zohar states:

> *Three drive the divine presence from this word and make it impossible for the Holy One, blessed is He, to fix His abode in the universe... And the [third] is one who destroys a fetus in the womb, for he destroys the craft of the Holy One, blessed be He, and his workmanship... on account of these abominations the Holy Spirit weeps...[1]*

Practically speaking, though, the approach to abortion is not so black-and-white. The eminent Rabbi Dr. Tzvi Hersh Weinreb, former CEO and Executive Vice President Emeritus of the Orthodox Union, accurately described the Torah approach as follows:

> *... in actual practice the Torah view of abortion is very different from the conservative views of the Catholic Church and from the liberal views of [many] Jewish groups. It is nuanced, complex, and depends upon such a variety of factors that categorizing Torah Judaism as either pro-life or pro-choice is almost a caricature of our position.[2]*

---

[1] *Zohar Shemos 3b.*

[2] "Orthodoxy in the Public Square" in *Tradition* 38:1 (Spring 2004), p. 34

Abortion is one of the few topics in the Noahide Laws for which there is extensive literature. The downside of so much being written is that even a cursory survey of the literature is far beyond the scope of this course.

A WARNING

Any practical questions of abortion <u>must</u> be asked to a competent _posek_. Issues of life and death cannot be determined by most Rabbis, <u>especially those who are experts in the Noahide laws.</u> The question must be asked to an impartial noted authority in Jewish Law [_posek_]. Any _posek_ capable of ruling on such issues will have expertise in the application of these laws to Noahides far beyond that of any expert or specialist in the Noahide laws.

Abortion in the Noahide Laws

Abortion falls under the category of murder within the Noahide laws. In Jewish law, abortion is also prohibited. However the details and sources of the prohibitions are different. They are so different that by studying the Jewish laws of abortion it is possible to come to the conclusion that killing a fetus is not murder for Noahides. The Talmud, however, teaches us that this is not so.

<u>Rebbi Yishmael</u>[3] makes an observation on the following verse:[4]

> One who spills the blood of man; by man shall his blood be spilt.

In Hebrew, this is an odd construction:

> Shofeikh dam ha-adam ba-adam damo yishafeikh

It is ambiguous, able to take a comma in two possible places. The first possibility is:

> Shofeikh dam ha-adam **,** ba-adam damo yishafeikh

Punctuated like this way, the verse yields the translation we have given above.

---

[3] <u>Sanhedrin 57b.</u>

[4] Gen. 9:6.

However, an alternate punctuation results in an altogether different meaning:

Shofeikh dam ha-adam ba-adam, damo yishafeikh

*One who spills the blood of a **person who is within a person**, his blood shall be spilt.*

Regarding this reading, the Talmud states:

> They [the sages] said in the name of Rebbi Yishmael: "Noahides are liable for killing a fetus. What is the reason for Rebbi Yishmael? For it states in the verse: 'One who spills the blood of a person who is within a person, his blood shall be spilt.' Which is a 'person who is within a person?' You would answer that this is a fetus."

The *halacha*, Torah law, follows the opinion of Rebbi Yishmael and the sages. Maimonides rules as such, writing:

> *A gentile who slays any soul, even a fetus in its mother's womb, is executed as penalty for its death.[5]*

At What Point Is Abortion Prohibited?

The contemporary political and religious debates on abortion have hinged upon the definition of embryonic/fetal life. This factor is the most important, yet by no means exclusive, consideration shaping the Torah's approach to the issue.

Abortion during the first 40 days following conception

The Talmud indicates in many places[6] that the embryo does not have the status of a "fetus" or a living being during the first 40 days following its conception. Rather, the embryo is termed *mayim bealma*, "only fluid." This is the *halacha*[7] and reflects a general principle that Torah law is not concerned with that which is microscopic or barely visible. At this stage in its development, the embryo has no *halachic*, practical, existence. Therefore, should a Jewish woman miscarry at this stage she is not subject to the impurity described in Leviticus 12:2-5.[8] As well, the spiritual impurities (*tumah*) associated with corpses are not assigned to a miscarried

---

[5] *Hilchos Melachim* 9:4.

[6] *Yevamos 69b*; *Niddah 30a*; *Bechoros 47b*.

[7] See *Shulchan Aruch* YD 305:23.

[8] See *Niddah* ibid.

embryo at this stage.[9] This fact allows for the possibility of abortion during the first 40 days.

However, life is not so simple – after all, it among the Holy One's greatest creations. The _Beer Halachos Gadolos_, one of the earliest and most important codes of Torah law, rules that a Jew may transgress Shabbat for the sake of saving an unborn life even during its first 40 days.[10]

The _Beer Halachos Gadolos_ obviously considers the embryo "alive enough" to permit a Jew to transgress Shabbat on its behalf. It appears that there are different definitions of life for different purposes of Torah law.

During the first 40 days after conception an embryo:

- Is not considered life for the laws of miscarriages,[11]
- Is not considered life for the laws of impurities caused by the dead,
- It is considered life enough to warrant violation of Shabbat in order to save it.

We must ask: Where is the threshold of life for the sake of the prohibition of abortion? This is a topic of **extensive** discussion.

Some _poskim_ have taken a very simple approach: if we are permitted to violate Shabbat to save the embryo, it must be prohibited at that point to abort the embryo. The _Chavas Yair_[12] writes that it doesn't make sense for Jews to be allowed to violate Shabbat to save a life that they could voluntarily terminate.

However, the reasons for permitting Shabbat violation for the life of the embryo may be more nuanced.

---

[9] _Mishneh LaMelekh_ to _Hilchos Tumas Meit_ 2:1.

[10] Cited in Nachmanides's _Toras HaAdam, Shaar HaSakanah_ II:29. _Rosh_ and _Ran_ also cite this as _halacha_ in their commentaries to _Yoma 82a_.

[11] As mentioned above.

[12] 31.

Human trafficking & abortion – what do they have in common?

Rashi[13] writes that the prohibition against selling someone into involuntary servitude applies even to an unborn child. Yet, the unborn child lacks full human status. Why then should it be included in this law?

Since the child will, as a matter of natural events, inevitably become fully human, it is treated as if fully human even at this point in its development.[14] Rav Issar Yehudah Unterman proposed[15] that this logic also underlies the *Beer Halachos Gadolos*'s permit to save an embryo during its first 40 days. In other words - the saving of *potential* life (an embryo during its first 40) is enough to warrant Jewish transgression of Shabbat.

According to this understanding, the fetus is not *actual*, yet only *potential* life during its first 40 days. Rav Unterman's thesis has significant support in earlier literature as well as from later *poskim*.

The implication of this approach for Noahides is important. From the Talmud's discussion of the Noahide prohibition of abortion, it is clear that Noahides are only liable for the taking of *actual* embryonic life, not *potential* embryonic life. This is indicated by the term *"a person within a person"* - one is only liable when the life of the fetus is comparable to that of the mother. Therefore, there may be no prohibition on Noahide abortion during the first 40 days after conception.

However, Rav Unterman's explanation is not accepted by all *poskim*.[16] Alone, it is not enough to permit abortion during the first 40 days. However, it is a significant factor when combined with other mitigating concerns.

Abortion When the Mother is Endangered

When a woman's life or health is put at serious risk by pregnancy, may the pregnancy be terminated? There are a number of factors to take into account, four of which are especially important:

1) Must a Noahide give her life rather than transgress?

---

[13] To Sanhedrin 85b.

[14] The idea that an object that will inevitably reach a state of obligation is considered in such a state even now is a principle occurring many times in Torah law.

[15] *Shevet MiYehudah* I:9.

[16] See notes to the summary below.

2) What is the status of the life of the embryo/fetus?

3) Does the law of *rodef*, a pursuer, apply to Noahides?

4) Is the embryo/fetus considered a *rodef*?

We will examine these four questions in no particular order.

Die or Transgress?

II Kings 5:14-19 records that Naaman (a Noahide) asked Elisha if he had committed a transgression when visiting his master, the King of Aram. The king had placed his hand upon Naaman, forcing him to bow down before an idol. Elisha replied: "Go in peace."

The Talmud, Sanhedrin 74b explains that Naaman's question was if he should have given his life rather than transgress. After all, the king had to force Naaman down with his own hands. Had Naaman resisted completely, he would have been risking his life! Elisha's reply, "go in peace," indicates that Naaman did nothing wrong. From this incident (involving idolatry no less!) the Talmud learns *a fortiori* that a Noahides has no obligation to give her life in lieu of transgressing any of her laws.[17] Therefore, a Noahide should be able to commit murder to save her life. By this reasoning, abortion is permitted to save the life of the mother (however, only the mother would be able to carry out the abortion, not another).

Does this apply to murder? The problem with this line of thought is that murder may be the exception to this rule. The Talmud, Sanhedrin 74a states as a logical fact that "no man's blood is redder than that of another." In other words: we do not make relative comparisons as to the values of individual lives.

Maimonides elaborates on this idea as it pertains to Jews in *Hilchos Yesodei HaTorah, Chapter 5*. The *Parshas Derakhim*[18] notes that Maimonides views this concept as a universal principle, applicable to Jews and non-Jews. This interpretation of Maimonides is corroborated by the Jerusalem Talmud, Shabbos 14 and Avodah Zarah 2:5.

---

[17] The Yad Ramah and Rashi had a slightly different version of the Talmud's text. According to their reading it comes out that a Noahide may be required to give up his life rather than transgress in public. Naaman, however, was permitted to bow because he was in private. However, Tosafos had a different reading in which Noahides are never required to give up their lives for their mitzvos. This latter reading is corroborated by most other Rishonim, including Rabbeinu Tam, Chiddushei HaRan, and Maimonides. It appears to be the one held as correct by most poskim.

[18] *Darsuh II, d.h. VeDah.*

They clearly view this idea as a logical principle applying to all mankind. Assuming this is so, a woman would <u>not</u> be permitted to abort (murder) the fetus to save her own life.

Yet, Maimonides, in discussing the Noahide laws, writes the following:

> *A gentile who is forced by another person to violate one of his commandments is permitted to transgress. Even if he is forced to worship false gods, he may worship them, **for gentiles are not commanded to sanctify God's name.**[19]*

Without making any distinctions, Maimonides permits a Noahide to transgress any of the Noahide laws when her life is in danger. Many authorities reject the *Parshas Derakhim*'s opinion based upon this passage, holding that Noahides may commit murder rather than suffer death (therefore permitting abortion to save the mother's life).[20]

The *Sefer Mitzvos HaShem* and other contemporary *poskim* have suggested a compromise of sorts. In the section quoted above Maimonides is only writing as about whether or not Noahides have a biblical obligation to give their life rather than transgress. This is why he writes "...**gentiles are not commanded to sanctify God's name.**" However, Maimonides in *Hilchos Yesodei HaTorah* teaches that there is a logical, yet non-biblical reason for Noahides to give their lives rather than transgress murder.

Many *poskim* agree with the *Parshas Drakhim*. Whether or not a Noahide must die rather than commit murder is too uncertain a matter to help us in the case at hand.

Rodef: The Pursuer

> *If a burglar is found tunneling into a home,*
> *and is discovered and killed, there is no liability.*
> Exodus 22:1

The Talmud, Sanhedrin 72a explains this verse. The assumption is the thief is armed and poses immediate danger to the residents of the house. Sanhedrin 73a cites further verses allowing, and even encouraging, the killing of one who poses immediate danger to another. This is known as the law of the *rodef*, the pursuer.

---

[19] Hilchos Melachim 10:2.

[20] The *Parshas Derakhim* states this as a possibility and cites those who hold accordingly. See *Maharash Yafeh* on *Bereshis Rabbah* 44:5. See also *Maskil LeDovid* on *Parshas Vayishlach*.

If a person is actively endangering the life of another, the one causing the danger must be neutralized by whatever means necessary.

We must ask two questions on this law:

1) Does the law of *rodef* apply to Noahides, and
2) In the case of a pregnancy, when the woman's life is endangered by the fetus, does the fetus have the *din*, law, of a *rodef*, a pursuer?

Does *rodef* apply to Noahides?

On the first question, the Talmud, Sanhedrin 57a appears to assume that the law of *rodef* applies to Noahides.[21] Most *poskim* concur, however they are uncertain as to who may kill the pursuer.[22] Is it permitted only for one being pursued, or is any onlooker permitted to kill the pursuer?

Is the fetus a *rodef*?

The Mishnah in *Ohalos* 7:6 states:

> *If a woman's labor endangers her life, the fetus must be cut up within her womb and removed piecemeal, for her life takes precedence over its life. If its greater part has already come forth, it must not be touched, for its life cannot supersede her life.*

The Mishnah does not tell us the reason for this ruling. However, the Talmud, discussing the law of the pursuer,[23] asks if a pursuer requires warning before he is killed. Along the way, they ask about our Mishnah, because a fetus cannot be warned:

> *Rav Chisda asked from the Mishnah: If a fetus is endangering the mother, we kill it. Once the head leaves the womb, we do not kill it. We do not kill one person to save another.*

> *[Answer:] That case is different. There, baby has no choice. Heaven is threatening the life of the mother.*

By asking if the fetus requires warning, the Talmud obviously assumes this is a case of a *rodef*, pursuer.

However, the Talmud's answer implies this is <u>not</u> a case of a pursuer because the baby has no intent nor is actively threatening the mother. Rather, the natural circumstances of birth are endangering the mother: "Heaven is threatening the life

---

[21] See *Minchas Chinuch* 296:5. While most *poskim* agree in principle, the details are hotly debated.

[22] See *Toldos Noach, Matza Chein* IV: 32 for an exhaustive overview of the sources.

[23] Sanhedrin 72b.

of the mother." The fetus is, apparently, only a tool to accomplish heaven's "pursuit."

Rashi, understands that *rodef*, the law of a pursuer, is not the operative permit for aborting the fetus (indeed, the Mishnah doesn't even mention it). Rashi writes that although the fetus is "alive enough" to render abortion prohibited, "as long as it has not emerged into the light of the world, it is not a [fully] human life." According to Rashi the value of the fetus's life does not trump that of the mother's; the mother's blood is redder than that of the fetus. This implies that the Talmud's dictum of not comparing life-to-life only applies to life that has fully emerged into this world. Once the head of the baby has emerged, it is considered fully human, equal to mother, and cannot be killed.

Maimonides learns that the fetus is a pursuer:

> *Our Sages ruled that when complications arise and a pregnant woman cannot give birth, it is permitted to abort the fetus in her womb, whether with a knife or with drugs,* **for the fetus is considered a rodef of its mother.** *If the head of the fetus emerges, it should not be touched, because one life should not be sacrificed for another. Although the mother may die, this is the nature of the world.*[24]

Why then does the emergence of the infant's head change the law according to Maimonides?

Many have explained that Maimonides views the life of the mother and infant as equal even before the head of the baby emerges. Therefore, unlike Rashi, there can be no permit to kill the fetus unless it is a pursuer.

The emergence of the head thus removes the law of "pursuer" from the baby. It appears that once the head has emerged, the infant is considered fully independent of the mother and cannot be considered a pursuer at that point.

The *Nodah BiYehudah*[25] and many others[26] have explained that the fetus is not actively "pursing" the woman, but is only a passive tool of heaven's pursuit. Once the head has emerged, the fetus is considered independent of the woman's body

---

[24] *Hilchos Rotzeach 1:9.*

[25] *Tinyana* CM 59.

[26] *Chavas Yoir* 31; *Chiddushei R' Chaim HaLevi, Rotzeach* 1:9. *Even HaAzel Rotzeach* 1:9 has a slightly altered understanding, however.

and it is only the circumstances of delivery, not the baby, that are endangering her life.

The Shulchan Aruch[27] establishes the Halacha like Maimonides. We should note, however, that there are numerous means of understanding Maimonides's reading of the Talmud. Some of these opinions have bizarre ramifications in Torah law and affect the laws for Noahides.[28]

See the summary with footnotes, below, for a practical overview of what emerges from this lesson.

Summary of the Lesson

1. During the first 40 days after conception, all agree that the "life" of the embryo is markedly different than after 40 days.

2. Therefore, in a case of even non-lethal medical risk to the mother, the pregnancy may be terminated at this stage.[29] Other situations (rape, incest, medical risks to the fetus, etc.) may also permit abortion at this stage.[30] However, they must be dealt with on a case-by-case basis bay a competent *posek*.

3. After 40 days, abortion of the fetus is considered murder in Noahide law.

---

[27] CM 452:2.

[28] There are some who prohibit abortions for Noahides under all conditions. However, these opinions are contrary to the majority of poskim. There are others who distinguish between cases of disease that endanger the pregnancy and danger resulting directly from the pregnancy. The following discuss the possible ramifications of Maimonides's reasoning on the halacha: Achiezer II:72; Sridei Eish III 342; Chemdas Yisrael, Maftechos ve-Hosafos p.32; Shu"t Koach Shor 20; Pachad Yitzchok (Lampronti), Erekh Nefalim 79b;

[29] R. Ovadiah Yosef, Yabi'a Omer, IV Even Ha-Ezer 1: 8-10 even permits abortions in such cases through the first trimester. See also Igros Moshe CM II:69 & 71. Seridei Eish I:162. See also Sheelas Yaavetz 43. This is an extremely controversial responsum, yet may be permitted for Noahides. See also Toras Chesed Even HaEzer 42:32. There are many who rule very severely on this issue, but the hanhaga of poskim today appears more lenient. See Levushei Mordekhai CM 36; Koach Shor 21.

[30] *Seridei Eish* ibid.

4. If the mother's life is endangered by the fetus during this period, abortion may be permitted. This is because the fetus is considered a *rodef*, a pursuer.

5. In cases of medical complications for the fetus or other factors (such as rape, incest, etc.) a *posek* must be consulted. Typically, the further along the pregnancy, the higher the risk standards must be to permit termination. If it is medically determined that the fetus will not live for 30 days after birth, abortion may also be permitted.[31]

6. For Noahides, there is uncertainty as to who may kill a *rodef*. If at all possible, the mother should herself use chemical or pharmaceutical methods (under the strict guidance and assistance of a physician) to terminate the pregnancy when permitted.

7. If the doctor must actively terminate the pregnancy (i.e. embryotomy), it is better that the mother use a Jewish rather than non-Jewish doctor. This is will be discussed more in the live lesson.

8. Once the head has emerged from the womb, the baby may not be harmed in any way.

---

[31] See *Hilchos Rotzeach* 2:6; *Maharam Shick* OH 142; *Minchas Chinuch* 34.

THE YESHIVA PIRCHEI SHOSHANIM SHULCHAN ARUCH LEARNING PROJECT

The Noahide Laws – Lesson Forty Two

164 Village Path, Lakewood NJ 08701 732.370.3344
164 Rabbi Akiva, Bnei Brak, 03.616.6340

Outline of This Lesson:

1. Introduction

2. Talmud *Yoma 28b*

3. Sanhedrin 59b

4. The Descendants of Keturah/Hagar

5. Voluntary Circumcision

6. Possibly Prohibited

7. Conclusions

8. Summary

Lifecycle V: Circumcision

Introduction

Circumcision is one of most well-known of Jewish obligations. Although Abraham and his household were commanded in circumcision, this has very little relevance to today's non-Jews. Nevertheless, may a Noahide elect to voluntarily circumcise himself? This is the topic of our lesson.

Talmud Sanhedrin 59b

Sanhedrin 59b discusses in detail the relevance of circumcision to Abraham, his household, and his descendants. The following summary is based upon Sanhedrin 59b and its commentaries.

Genesis 17:10 – 13 states:

> *This is My covenant that you shall keep between Me,* **you,** *and* **your offspring after you***: every male* **among you** *shall be circumcised. You shall be circumcised in the flesh of your foreskin and it shall be a token of the covenant between Me and you. He* **among you** *that is eight days old shall be circumcised, every male throughout* **your** *generations that is* **born in your house** *… He that is born in your house… must be circumcised; and My covenant shall be in your flesh for an everlasting covenant.*

The Torah is very specific in commanding circumcision only to Abraham, his household, and his offspring. In the first generation of this commandment, it applied only to Abraham, Isaac, and Ishmael. However, Genesis 21:12 later states:

> *Whatever Sarah tells you, heed her voice, since through Isaac will your offspring considered yours.*

We see that only Isaac and his offspring were, in distinction to Ishmael, considered heirs to Abraham's spiritual legacy. Therefore, circumcision was only obligatory for the descendants of Isaac. Similarly, Isaac said to Jacob:

And God will give to you and your descendants the blessings of Abraham.[1]

We see from here that God designated Jacob, not Esau, as the heir to the Abrahamic legacy of which circumcision was the sign. Those descendants of Jacob/Israel are the Jewish people of today.

The Descendants of Keturah/Hagar

The Torah states:

*Vayosef Abraham and took a wife whose name was **Keturah**.*[2]

The Midrash[3] and Torah commentaries[4] note two anomalies in this verse. The first is the word *Vayosef*, which is a strange construction for introducing marriage, implying "gathering in" or "adding."[5] Furthermore, Keturah is not a proper name, but a title meaning "restrained" or "controlled." Some commentaries also interpret the name as a reference to *ketores*, incense, meaning that she and her deeds were pleasing. The Midrash explains that Abraham remarried Hagar, taking her again as his wife. Hagar had remained faithful to Abraham, reconciling with him following the death of Sarah.

Abraham and Hagar produced six children from this union (see Gen. 25:2). The commentaries explain that these children and their descendants were obligated in circumcision. After all, they were born into Abraham's home and, unlike Ishmael and Esau, were never actually excluded from the command of circumcision.[6]

The descendants of these children eventually intermarried with the descendants of Ishmael to the point that they are indistinguishable from the Ishmaelites.

---

[1] Gen. 28:4.

[2] Gen. 25:1.

[3] *Tanchuma* 5; *Bereshis Rabbah* 61:4.

[4] *Rashi*; *Ramban*; many others to this verse.

[5] See *Targumim*.

[6] See the *Malbim* and *Zohar* who discuss the differences between Ishmael and these siblings.

Therefore, the modern Ishmaelites, those of paternal Arab ancestry, are obligated in circumcision.[7] Maimonides summarizes the Talmud's conclusions in *Hilchos Melachim* 10:7-8:

> *§7 Only Abraham and his descendants were commanded in circumcision, as Genesis 17:9-10 states: "Keep My covenant, you and your offspring... you shall circumcise every male." The descendants of Ishmael are excluded by Genesis 21:12: "It is through Isaac, that your offspring will be called." Esau's descendants are also excluded, for Isaac told Jacob in Genesis 28:4: "May God grant Abraham's blessing to you and your descendants," implying that only he is the true offspring of Abraham who maintained his faith and his righteous behavior. Thus, they alone are obligated in circumcision.*

> *§8 Our Sages related that the descendants of Keturah, who are the offspring of Abraham that came after Isaac and Ishmael, are also obligated in circumcision. At present, the descendants of Ishmael have become intermingled with the descendants of Keturah. Therefore, they are all obligated to be circumcised on the eighth day.*

May A Noahide Voluntarily Undergo Circumcision?

The Talmud teaches:

Rabbah Bar Bar Chanaha said in the name of Rabbi Yochanan: a ger toshav *who allows 12 months to pass without circumcising himself is like any other idolater. [The Sages responded:] That is in a case when he vowed to circumcise himself and failed to do so.[8]*

Explanation: this case is of a non-Jew who, when accepting the seven Noahide laws to become a *ger toshav*, voluntarily vows to circumcise himself. If he hasn't done so after 12 months, we assume that his vow was insincere. If he was insincere at the time of his vow, we must also doubt his sincerity in accepting the Noahides laws.[9]

We learn a number of things from this passage. For one, it appears that a *ger toshav* may circumcision himself. We also see that circumcision is voluntary – a *ger toshav* is certainly <u>not</u> obligated to circumcise himself.

---

[7] The minimum of circumcision required to fulfill this commandment is different than for Jews. While Jews must remove the entire foreskin, the Bnei Keturah fulfill this mitzvah with the removal of the outer foreskin. See *Shaagas Aryeh*; *Minchas Chinuch* 2.

[8] <u>Avodah Zarah 65a.</u>

[9] See commentaries to *Avodah Zarah* ibid.

Maimonides writes in his discussion of *ger toshav*:

> **Anyone** *who agrees to circumcise himself and allows twelve months to pass without doing so is considered an idolater.* [10]

In contradistinction to the rest of the section, Maimonides applies the Talmud's statement to "**anyone**." Shall we understand this to mean that the Talmud's statement is not unique to *ger toshav*, but applies to any non-Jew who accepts the Noahide laws? If it applied to "anyone," even modern Noahides, then who exactly "considers him an idolater?"

Also, when is this "vow to circumcise himself" made? Is it connected to the acceptance of the obligation of the Noahide laws, or is it talking about any religiously motivated circumcision? Perhaps, we are reading too much into Maimonides. Perhaps "anyone" should be read in context, meaning any *ger toshav*. Even in this case, though, it may be that circumcision is permitted to any Noahide.

Each possibility leads to a variety of possible conclusions that we will summarize shortly.

Possibly Prohibited?

Rabbenu Yerucham[11] *paskened*, decided, that it is prohibited to circumcise a non-Jew for any reason other than conversion to Judaism. The Rama agrees and cites this as the *halacha*, law, in the Shulchan Aruch.[12] Additionally, we note that a Jew may circumcise a non-Jew for medical purposes.[13] Taking these two *halachos* together, it appears that a Jew is precluded from circumcising a Noahide for religious purposes. Yet, if Noahides may practice circumcision (as the Talmud certainly implies), then why would it be prohibited for Jews to assist them?

The *poskim* who come after the Rama are very uncertain as to the reason for this law and details of its application. Indeed, it poses a number of contradictions to other statements in the Talmud and *poskim*.[14] It is possible that the source is from

---

[10] *Hilchos Melachim* 8:10.

[11] In his *Toldos Adam VeChavah*, cited in *Bais Yosef* at the end of YD 266.

[12] *Yoreh Deah* 263:5.

[13] See *Avodah Zarah 26b* with the comments of the *Chiddushei HaRitva, Rashi,* and *Tosafos*. See *Otzar HaBris* I p.59 in the *Ohalei Shem. Shulchan Aruch paskens* such in YD 268:9.

[14] Many of the *nosei kelim* on *Shulchan Aruch*, both on YD 263:5 and 268:9, debate the reasons. The Taz holds that by assisting a non-Jew the Jew is nullifying circumcision as a sign of the covenant. This would present a basis for prohibiting Noahide circumcision. However, it is not clear that the

the *Zohar*,[15] which writes that Joseph sinned by encouraging the Egyptians to adopt circumcision. This was despite Joseph's intent being for the sake of heaven. However, it appears that these were forced circumcisions, which would be prohibited in any case.

Conclusions

There does not appear to be any reason in Torah literature to assume that Noahides are prohibited from circumcising themselves. To the contrary, it appears that circumcision was a sign of commitment to the creator even before Abraham was commanded in it. After all, the Midrash[16] states that Adam, Shes, and Noah all came into the world circumcised, attaching special significance to this.

Furthermore, if there was a prohibition on Noahides practicing circumcision, then the prohibition would upon them, and not as a prohibition upon Jews against circumcising them.

It seems that the Talmud permits any Noahide to voluntarily circumcise himself. Maimonides, citing the Talmud, does so only for the issue of trusting a *ger toshav's* acceptance of the Noahide laws. There is no reason to assume that there should be any difference here between Noahides and *ger toshav*. There are further reasons to permit voluntary circumcision to Noahides that will be discussed in the live class.

It is possible to object to Noahide circumcision based on the prohibition against wounding oneself. However, it does not appear that voluntary circumcision would fall under this prohibition.[17]

Although Noahides may voluntarily circumcise themselves, using a Jewish doctor or *mohel*, circumciser, may present problems for the Jew.

Taz himself would oppose Noahide circumcision (this will be discussed in the live lesson). It is possible that this logic would have prohibited Noahide circumcision before matan Torah, yet not afterwards. See also Levush; Meil Tzedaka 14:2; Otzar HaBris ibid. for further discussion of the underlying reasons.

[15] *Miketz.*

[16] *Tanhuma Noach* 6:5.

[17] For perspectives on this issue, see *Panim Yafos* to *Lech Lecha*; *HaMikneh*, end of *Kiddushin*; *Gliyoni Shas* (Engil) to Avodah Zarah 10b; *Meshech Chochmah Vayishlach* 34:22.

This is because of the prohibition of a Jew circumcising a gentile.[18] In such a case, the *mohel* or doctor may decline.

We will discuss practical aspects and reasons for voluntary Noahide circumcision more in the live lesson.

Summary of This Lesson

1. Noahides have no obligation in circumcision.

2. However, those of paternal Arab ancestry may be obligated in circumcision because of being *Bnei Keturah*.

3. Voluntary circumcision appears permitted to Noahides for reasons that will be discussed in the live class.

4. However, there is a prohibition prohibiting a Jew from circumcising a non-Jew. The reasons for this prohibition are very unclear. However, it seems unrelated to the question of whether or not a Noahide may voluntarily undergo circumcision.

---

[18] Although it is possible to find room for leniency (especially based upon the *Shach*, however his views are problematic, as proven by the *nekudas hakesef*), most *poskim* are conservative. See *Shu"t Har Tzvi* YD 215; *Minchas Yitzchok* I:36.

Made in the USA
Columbia, SC
20 March 2022

57911326R10128